ANTIQUARIES, BOOK COLLECTORS
AND THE CIRCLES OF LEARNING

PUBLISHING PATHWAYS

ANTIQUARIES, BOOK COLLECTORS AND THE CIRCLES OF LEARNING

Edited by
Robin Myers and Michael Harris

ST PAUL'S BIBLIOGRAPHIES

WINCHESTER

OAK KNOLL PRESS

DELAWARE

© 1996 The Contributors

First published 1996 by
St Paul's Bibliographies
West End House
1 Step Terrace
Winchester
Hampshire SO22 5BW

Published in North and South America
and the Philippines by
Oak Knoll Press
414 Delaware Street
New Castle
DE 19720

ISBN 1-873040-29-6 (UK)
ISBN 1-884718-24-8 (USA)

Library of Congress Cataloging-in-Publication Data

Antiquaries, book collectors, and the circles of learning / edited by Robin
Myers and Michael Harris.
      p.   cm. -- (Publishing pathways)
    Includes index.
    ISBN 1-884718-24-8
    1. Book collecting--Great Britain--History--Congresses.
2. Society of Antiquaries of London--History--Congresses. 3. Great
Britain--Historiography--Congresses. I. Myers, Robin. II. Harris,
M. (Michael). 1938- III. Series.
Z987.5.07A68 1996
381'.45002'0941--dc20   96-29140
                                              CIP

Typeset in Times by Ella Whitehead, Munslow, Shropshire
Cover designed by Eric Dent
Printed in England by St Edmundsbury Press, Bury St Edmunds

Contents

Contributors

JANET BACKHOUSE is Curator of Illuminated Manuscripts at the British Library and is Fellow of the Society of Antiquaries. She has lectured and written extensively on medieval books.

T. A. BIRRELL is a retired teacher of English, and is presently engaged in compiling a catalogue of the Old Royal Library. His publications include *The Library of John Morris* and *English Monarchs and their Books*.

CHRISTOPHER DE HAMEL is Senior Director of Sotheby's, London and a Fellow of the Society of Antiquaries. He is the author of, among other works, *A History of Illuminated Manuscripts* (new ed. 1994) and *Scribes and Illuminators*.

MIRJAM FOOT is Director of Collections and Preservation at the British Library. She is well known for her extensive writing on the history of bookbinding and allied subjects.

ARNOLD HUNT is a research fellow at Trinity College, Cambridge. His article on Richard Heber and Charles Henry Hartshorne was published in the *Book Collector* in 1993.

ROBIN MYERS is co-founder of the Publishing Pathways conferences and co-editor of the published proceedings. She is President of the Bibliographical Society and Hon Archivist of the Stationers' Company of London. She has written widely on many aspects of the history of the book trade.

BERNARD NURSE is Librarian at the Royal Society of Antiquaries, London.

DAVID PEARSON is Head of Acquisitions at the National Art Library, Victoria and Albert Museum. He previously worked at the British Library and is Secretary to the Bibliographical Society. His most recent book is *Provenance Research in Book History*.

Introduction

THE ORGANIZATION of learning in England has always depended on liaisons within 'the republic of letters'. The formal centres of culture, above all the ancient universities of Oxford and Cambridge, were involved in the development of a number of learned institutions emanating from London. The Royal Society in the seventeenth century and the Society of Antiquaries in the eighteenth became the focus of many areas of scientific and historical investigation. Other 'institutions' for social and cultural intercourse developed in towns and cities outside the metropolis, some with regular meetings in a club open to members or, by invitation, in a private house. Beyond these closed confederacies of scholars and antiquaries, with their networks of communication, shifting patterns of informal association created by shared interests in study and collecting formed widening circles of individuals and groups. Some of these seekers after learning met sporadically, others communicated only in writing, but always the correspondence that ran round the circuits linking friends and acquaintances provided a framework for shared activity in pursuit of learning; and, whether circulating in manuscript or print, in volume or in serial form it was publication which gave shape and meaning to the diffuse activity of individuals and organizations and provided the basic mechanism for the sharing of ideas and information. The collector, eagerly accumulating books and manuscripts as well as archaeological finds and 'curiosities', had an important rôle in providing a scholarly resource. In his tireless search (though today we would condemn some of it as destructive) he contributed to the process of identification and organization, even if some of it only came to light when it was dispersed in the saleroom or through booksellers' catalogues.

The contributors to this volume view the world of learning from different angles and provide original accounts of the way it worked in the fields of literature, architecture and textual study. None is concerned with scientific antiquarianism, and their focus is the Society of Antiquaries rather than the Royal Society, even though the eighteenth-century antiquary made little distinction between the two and, as in the case of Andrew Ducarel, a man might be fellow of both. The papers fall into three groups; Mirjam Foot and David Pearson consider the connection between scholars and their books as demonstrated by the visible characteristics of their bindings; Tom Birrell, Arnold Hunt and Robin Myers concentrate on an individual collector or antiquary; and Janet Backhouse and Christopher de Hamel chart the transfer of great manuscripts and the dismantling of a manuscript collection on the grand scale. All, however, intersect at certain points, thus emphasizing the continual interaction within the world of learning.

David Pearson describes, in detail, some of the books which were owned by scholars and are now preserved in Oxford libraries. His examination of the bindings produced between 1550 and 1650 shews that scholars were hardly ever interested in their books as physical objects. Plain, durable and largely unadorned, the bindings provide a striking example of the triumph of use over fashion. Mirjam Foot takes the longer view and spreads her net over three centuries, considering the way that the wealthy scholar and aristocratic European collector was concerned with the outward appearance of his books. With taste and money to spend in the service of learning, he assembled a library of handsome books decorated with the care and attention to detail needed for them both to look well on the shelves and to be serviceable; though this could not always be achieved without some acrimonious bickering between patron and binder.

Tom Birrell, Arnold Hunt and Robin Myers consider individuals whose antiquarian or collecting interests led to the development of the circles of learning. Andrew Ducarel in the eighteenth century and John Gage in the nineteenth were antiquaries in both senses of the word; they were students of the antique and were influential members of the Society of Antiquaries of London. Robin Myers gives an account of Andrew Ducarel's life and that aspect of his work which was concerned with the study of Anglo-Norman culture and ecclesiastical architecture by the comparative method, which had not previously been looked at in this way. John Gage, the early nineteenth-century Director of the Society of Antiquaries, who is the subject of Tom Birrell's paper, provides a fit sequel to Ducarel in that he helped to take medieval studies into the nineteenth century; Gage's particular bent, his tastes and Catholic gentry background, chimed well with the Society's current interest in the publication of Anglo-Saxon texts with translation *en face*. Tom Birrell's account of Gage's edition for the Society of the Luttrell Psalter links his contribution with that of Janet Backhouse whose paper follows chronologically with an account of the deposit and eventual acquisition by the British Museum of this manuscript in the late 1920s. Arnold Hunt is concerned to exemplify, in his account of Richard Heber's life and library, the early nineteenth-century taste in book-collecting in the service of literature, at a time, as he puts it, when 'the bibliographical was political' and Heber's being a distinguished book collector could win Earl Spencer's political support. Arnold Hunt's account of Heber as the study of one man and his influence, has links with Tom Birrell's and Robin Myers's papers as well as with Mirjam Foot's account of the collecting philosophy of a bibliophile in the service of scholarship. It contrasts with the attitude of David Pearson's Oxford scholars who were concerned to assemble working libraries. Janet Backhouse's and Christopher de Hamel's collectors owned manuscripts of a magnificence that would have been beyond the reach of any of the other collectors or antiquaries discussed. Both deal with dispersal or transfer, rather than the process of assembly. Janet Backhouse tells a story, hitherto buried in the British Museum's archive and permitted to be brought into the open for the first time. In 1896, a pair of pre-eminent English manuscripts, the Luttrell Psalter and the Bedford Book of Hours, were put on deposit at the British Museum by the Weld family who owned them; but in 1929, when the family had urgently to raise money for death duties, they were suddenly removed. Janet Backhouse tells how (but it is a moot point whether anyone comes out of it very well) they were eventually secured for the Museum and the nation after a good deal of dubious 'backstage diplomacy' and, on the part of the vendors, by nefarious practices or 'blatant manipulation' which make entertaining reading after the passage of more than 60 years. Baron Edmond de Rothschild's superb collection of manuscripts, in contrast, was international both as regards its content and the way it was assembled, but it was almost a secret collection, without catalogue or photographic record. The unifying factor was that all the manuscripts in the collection were late-medieval and had fantastic royal provenances. Its dispersal, first by inheritance and then by looting during the Second World War, is dramatically told by Christopher de Hamel whose detailed detective work and documentation, in text and footnotes, will add a useful resource for scholars seeking the present whereabouts of some of the manuscripts.

Finally, Bernard Nurse's history of the library of the Society of Antiquaries, which at the conference was followed by a visit to the library itself, provides a suitable coda to those studies of antiquaries and collectors, many of whom enriched the Society's library and their circles of learning.

Michael Harris
Robin Myers
London
July 1996

Acknowledgements

The 1995 conference on the history of the book trade, held under the auspices of the Centre for Extra Mural Studies, Birkbeck College, University of London, took place at the Society of Antiquaries, Burlington House, a fitting location for this particular conference, the eighteenth in the series. Five of the seven contributors are themselves Fellows of the Society.

We are grateful, yet again, to the Marc Fitch Trust for generously assisting us with the cost of extra illustrations to this, the sixteenth volume in the Publishing Pathways series. We are grateful to all who supplied photographs for reproduction. We extend special thanks to the Alice Trust, Waddesdon Manor, for supplying a photograph of Baron Edmond de Rothschild and for generously waiving a reproduction fee.

List of those attending the Conference

R. Amati
Collector, London

Jean Archibald
Edinburgh University Library

Bernadette Archer
*National Art Library, Victoria &
Albert Museum*

Dr Marie Axton
*English Faculty, University of
Cambridge*

Chiara Barontini
*Curator, Victoria & Albert
Museum*

Ulrich Bach
*M.A. student, History of the
Book, London*

Dr William Baker
*Department of English,
Northern Illinois University*

Melanie Barber
*Archivist, Lambeth Palace
Library*

Philippa Bernard
Bookseller, Chelsea Rare Books

Bill Bell
*Department of English, Edin-
burgh University*

Fiona Black
*Librarian, Regina, Canada &
research student, University of
Loughborough*

Iain Brown
*M.A. student, History of the
Book, University of London*

Gillis Burgess
Charity officer, London

John Cherry
*Secretary, Society of Antiquaries
of London*

Paul Christianson
*Professor of English, Wooster
College, Ohio*

Andrew Cook
Archivist, India Office Library

Karen Cook
*Curator, British Library Map
Library*

Robert Cross
*Publisher, St Paul's
Bibliographies*

Keri Davies
*Librarian, Enfield & M.A.
student, History of the Book,
London*

Lucy Dean
*Library & M.A. student, History
of the Book, London*

Catherine Devas
Bibliophile

Felix de Marez Oyens
New York

Roger de Kesel
Bibliophile, Belgium

Sarah Dodgson
*Librarian, the Athenaeum,
London*

Carlo Dumontet
National Art Library, London

Naomi Dungworth
*Curator, Victoria & Albert
Museum*

Keith Fletcher
Antiquarian bookseller, London

Richard Ford
Antiquarian bookseller, London

Sam Fogg
Antiquarian bookseller, London

Sir Angus Fraser
Retired civil servant

Helmut Friedlaender
Book collector, New York City

Janet Ing Freeman
Bibliographer

Dr Jacqueline Glomski
*Assistant librarian, Warburg
Institute*

Elizabeth Godbeer
*Documentation officer, Old
Speech Room Gallery, Harrow
School*

Ann Goldgar
*Department of History, King's
College, London*

Denise Harrison

David J. Hall
Cambridge University Library

Richard Hatchwell
*Antiquarian bookseller,
Malmesbury*

Frank Herrman
*Bloomsbury Book Auctions &
author*

John Hewish
Retired librarian

Christopher Hill

Sandra Hindman
*Professor of History,
Northwestern University, USA*

Sheila Hingley
*Librarian, Canterbury Cathedral
Library*

Paul Hopkins
*Spencer archivist,
Northamptonshire Record
Office*

A. W. Huish
Retired librarian

Lynn Hulse
*Research fellow, Portland
Library*

Mervyn Jannetta
Curator, The British Library

David Katz
*Faculty of Humanities, Tel Aviv
University, Israel*

Victor Keats

Patrick King
Bookseller, Stony Stratford

Colin Lee
*Collector, and Treasurer,
Heraldry Society*

J. D. Lee
Indexer and bibliographer

Brian North Lee
Book-plate collector & author

Elizabeth Leedham-Green
Cambridge University Library

Yvonne Lewis
*Assistant Adviser, National
Trust libraries*

Peter Lucas
*Visiting Fellow, Corpus College,
Cambridge*

Warren McDougall
*Bibliographer & book collector,
Edinburgh*

Christina Mackwell
*Librarian, Lambeth Palace
Library*

Giles Mandelbrote
Curator, The British Library

George Mandl
Paper maker

Rovianne Matovu
Research student

Gordon Milne
*Bookbinding student,
Roehampton*

J. G. Morgan

Laura Nuvoloni
*PhD student, King's College,
London*

Charles Parry
National Library of Wales

Diana Patterson
*Bibliographer & instructor,
Mount Royal College, Calgary,
Alberta*

Margaret Payne
Librarian, Kent

Michael Perkin
*Reading University &
Winchester Cathedral libraries*

Esther Potter
Retired librarian

Nicholas Poole-Wilson
Bookseller, Bernard Quaritch

Dorine Proske van Hendt
Art historian, Amsterdam

Nigel Ramsay
*Curator, British Library
Department of Manuscripts*

Monica Schertzer

Martin Schoyen
*Schoyen manuscript collection,
Oslo*

Alison Shell
*Research fellow, University
College, London*

Michael Silverman
Autograph dealer, London

Julianne Simpson
*Librarian, University of Oxford
Early Book Project*

Elizabeth Sorenssen
*Librarian, Schoyen Collection,
Oslo*

Beryl Stevens

David Stoker
University of Wales, Aberystwyth

Dinah Swayne
Bookbinder & conservator

Thomas Symonds
Publisher, Pindar Press

Anthony Taussig

Jean Tsushima
Archivist, HAC & historian

Ruby Reid Thompson
*Archivist Portland Library,
Literary Manuscripts*

Veronica Watts
Bookseller

John Walwyn-Jones
Bookseller, Questor Rare Books

Alexis Weedon
Lecturer, Luton University

Eva Weininger
Collector, courtesy literature

K. D. Wigin
Bibliophile

Ian Willison
*Senior Research Fellow, Centre
for English Studies, University
of London*

John Wilson
Bibliophile

Laurence Worms
Bookseller, Ash Rare Books

Peter Wright
Retired lecturer in librarianship

William Zachs
Edinburgh University

Scholars and bibliophiles:
book collectors in Oxford, 1550–1650

DAVID PEARSON

THIS PAPER is intended to address a series of related questions connected with the history of book collecting in the late sixteenth and early seventeenth centuries, which have not been extensively or systematically explored before. Its purpose is to ask: to what extent were British book-owners of this period interested in their books as physical objects? Were they concerned with the ways their books were bound, and, if so, what were the features which concerned them? Do the ways in which they marked their books tell us anything about the way they regarded them? How far was their approach to the books an aesthetic one, and how far was it a purely functional or textual one? To put it another way, were these collectors bibliophiles, or book accumulators? My exploration of these questions will be based very largely on the observations I made during a research project which involved working round the college libraries of Oxford, investigating the development of Oxford bookbinding between about 1500 and 1640. It is, therefore, very Oxford-centred, but Oxford is not a bad place on which to focus. It was one of the three major hives of bookbinding activity in England, along with Cambridge and London, and it housed continuous and successive generations of book owners throughout the defined period, and indeed throughout all periods from the middle ages to the present day.

We do not have a proper narrative history of book collecting in this country, which takes an all-round view of all kinds of collectors from all periods. The nearest thing we have is de Ricci's *English collectors of books and manuscripts* (1930), which is probably the book that will spring most rapidly to mind to counter this allegation, but de Ricci concentrates very much on the top end of the market and on the period from 1700 onwards; his coverage of centuries before the eighteenth is too patchy to be taken seriously. There is however a generally accepted understanding of the development of book collecting, which runs something like this. Medieval private libraries were normally quite small affairs, restricted by the high cost of manuscript books to the more affluent members of society. The introduction of printing and a gradual increase in literacy made private book ownership possible on a more generous scale, and from the sixteenth century onwards we see collections of books being owned more widely by academics, clergymen, antiquaries, and people on all points of the social scale from merchants to aristocrats. The biggest libraries get gradually bigger and each generation sees the accumulation of larger and larger collections by those who have the means and the inclination. The motivating forces behind the development of these collections may be varied, but they are more associated with practicality than connoisseurship: the need to have at hand the necessary texts for the completion of one's studies, or to write one's books, or to confute the arguments of one's academic or theological opponents; the desire to have books to read; the desire to amass the totality of available knowledge on particular subjects. There are the great antiquaries and manuscript collectors like Matthew Parker and Robert Cotton, but they too had very practical goals; they saw the need to preserve historical evidence and Parker certainly saw his early manuscript texts playing a role in the defence of the Elizabethan church settlement. It is around the turn of the eighteenth century that new currents in book collecting are thought to emerge: as de Ricci put it, 'it was about the year 1700 that several members of the British nobility became simultaneously seized with a violent desire to collect incunabula'.[1] From then on we can see the steady development of the vogue for collecting books because they are rare, or because they are beautiful, or because they are objects of taste and fashion. This is not to say that the older motives for the owning of books did not continue to operate, as they do to this day; it is more accurate to posit that the reasons for book collecting broadened out than to suggest that they underwent a fundamental change. Both Matthew Parker and J. R. Abbey had fine and handsome bindings, but their reasons for owning them were different. The idea of collecting bindings for their own sake, and because the history of decorated bookbinding was a subject worth studying, would have been totally alien to Parker and other collectors of his generation.

This study is not primarily concerned with collectors of the status of Parker, but with men of more modest, though not negligible, means whose collecting activities were largely or wholly Oxford-based through their attachment to the University. The college libraries of Oxford contain many collections of this period, given or bequeathed by the men who put them together, and which often survive more or less intact to this day. They may be small and scattered among the bookstacks, like the 38 books given to Oriel by John Jackman in 1599, or large and accessible *en bloc*, like the 2000-odd volumes given to Wadham by Philip Bisse shortly before he died in 1614, which have recently been united as a group on the Library shelves. *In toto* they are fairly representative of the kinds of books which were circulating among and owned by private individuals in Oxford in great numbers. We know, from the evidence of the probate inventories which are increasingly being made available through the editorial activities of *Private libraries in Renaissance England*, that book ownership was widespread, and that late sixteenth-century Oxford academics commonly had collections of anything between 20 and 300 volumes.[2]

There are a number of general observations that can be made about academic life at this time, and the place of books within that life. The first thing to remember is that the average level of material possessions was much lower than we are used to today. James McConica, who writes about the domestic conditions of the Oxford colleges in the sixteenth-century volume of the *History of the University of Oxford*, reminds us that 'life in the Elizabethan college was undoubtedly spartan and severe'.[3] He paints a picture of a lifestyle which, by twentieth-century standards, is both uncouth and uncomfortable, of unheated and sparsely furnished rooms shared as living quarters by several students at a time. There are contemporary testimonies to the miseries of college life in winter, such as the mid sixteenth-century anecdote that Cambridge students had to spend half an hour running up and down before retiring for the night 'to gette a heate on their feete whan they go to bed'.[4] I was struck by an inscription in a grammatical text book in Jesus College Library, dated 1568, which reads 'George Dorrell oweth this booke witnesse of John Porter his bedfellow': it seems to bear eloquent and direct testimony of the realities of sixteenth-century student life.[5] The point which is relevant to my theme is not the level of discomfort but the level of material possessions. The average student or professional academic of today is likely to possess a greater and wider range of objects than his sixteenth-century counterpart. He is likely to be able to manifest any wish to express individuality or create an environment in line with his aesthetic desires in a greater variety of ways. We might expect, therefore, that a sixteenth-century owner who possessed books but relatively little else might take a proportionately greater interest in the cherishing of those books as physical objects. I put this forward simply as an idea to consider in what follows.

Contemporary portraits provide a medium which demonstrates the centrality of books to the life of university men. Painted or engraved portraits of sixteenth-century individuals frequently incorporate icons of things which are dear to them or symbolize their activities. Thus portraits of Francis Drake show him holding the globe which he circumnavigated, and portraits of statesmen sometimes show them holding bunches of papers and documents.[6] In the case of scholars the object, not surprisingly, is a book. A portrait of John Rainolds, president of Corpus in the first decade of the seventeenth century, a man whose extensive book collection is now scattered around Oxford and elsewhere, displays a book as a prominent feature of the overall composition. Thomas James, Bodley's first librarian, was depicted holding a book to his chest in a protective sort of way. Bodley himself is positively imprisoned between towers of books in his memorial in Merton College Chapel. Laurence Humfrey, in his monument in Magdalen College, is holding out a book in an inviting way. Edmund Grindal, whose books went to Queen's, is seen clutching a book in a portrait of him now at Canterbury.[7] Mrs Poole's catalogue of portraits in the Oxford colleges reveals time and again this inclusion of books, this testimony to the book as something inescapable from their lives and symbolic of their activities.[8]

The ownership of books in Tudor and Stuart Oxford was facilitated and made possible by the existence of a flourishing book trade, which organized the selling of new and second-hand books, the importing of newly published books from London and abroad, the binding and rebinding of books, and also, from 1585 onwards, the printing of books. It is not the purpose of this study to explore the precise interrelationships between these various operations, which is complicated and largely uncharted territory, but just to make some general observations about the binding side and the ways in which it made choices available to customers. The bookbinders of Oxford worked entirely in accordance with the practices of their period, and at any one time there were numerous binders operating simultaneously who were capable of producing a range of work, both decoratively and structurally, from the simple to the more sophisticated. They could produce limp vellum bindings, leather over pasteboard, leather over wood, and they could decorate the covers more or less elaborately. We do not actually know very much about the cheap end of the market, because so little has survived, but we can confidently surmise that it was active. The decorative options were dictated by the fashion of the day, but the essential principle of a range of choice remained; at the end of the century, for example, Oxford bookbuyers could have their bindings decorated with rolls, or centrepieces, to varying degrees of elaboration. To what extent, and in what ways, were these various choices exercised by the customers? To what extent do they appear to have ordered or selected their books with decorative or aesthetic concerns in mind? A related question follows from the observation that decorative styles changed as the decades passed. As rolls and pineapples gave way to rolls and Renaissance fleurons, as different layout patterns were introduced, as centrepieces came and went – to what extent, if any, were these changes dictated or influenced by customer preference? What is the motor for change in the decorative fashions of bookbindings?

I think that this question – why do decorative tastes change? – is one of the hardest to deal with. It is not related to bookbinding specifically, but to the wider history of every kind of decorated artefact, a broad stream of which bookbindings are one small current. The answer must ultimately lie in some fundamental and general aspect of human behaviour, easy to observe but less easy to explain, and it is not an area in which I am competent or eager to theorize. One thing I do not believe is that the bookbinders played a very active role in this process – I do not think they were responsible either for tool design or for experimenting with it and developing it. Nor do I think that the customers had much to do with it. We do not of course know who *did* design the tools – whether it was the metalsmiths who cut them or an artist-draughtsman whose designs were duly copied – but my own mental picture of the way it worked does not include the bookbinder going into the goldsmith's shop with a drawing and saying 'make me something like that'. While it is observable that decorative fashions change, it is equally observable that at any one time most bookbinding shops had sets of tools which looked very similar, and that they deployed those tools in pretty much the same ways. Fig.1 shows an Oxford binding of about 1595 decorated with a centrepiece whose design was a popular one; in the late sixteenth and early seventeenth centuries there were nine variants of this centrepiece pattern in use there.[9] Despite their close similarities they all have individual features and it is easy to tell them apart once you have your eye in. There cannot be any doubt that they

Fig.1. R. Bellarmino, *Disputationum . . . de controversiis Christianae fidei . . . tomus secundus*, Ingolstadt, 1589. Bound in Oxford c.1590-95. *Private collection.*

are copied from the same design idea, and the chronology of use makes it likely that some were cloned in Oxford from ones already in use. They were not owned by the same workshop but were distributed around the several different binders who all used them to produce bindings looking like the one shown in fig.1. Sorting out the binding workshops of Oxford at this time, and drawing the clear boundary lines between them that binding historians like to draw, is not actually as easy as one would like it to be, but in the middle decades of the sixteenth century it is possible to identify three particular tool groupings which apparently correspond to different workshops. They all used rolls as their primary device for decorating leather bindings and they all laid them out in very similar ways. Basil Oldham, in his standard work on sixteenth-century English roll bindings, maps out some of the design layouts which are often characteristic of different binding centres and he rightly notes that a pattern of a saltire within a rectangular frame is often an Oxford binding. Fig.2 shows three bindings from these three workshops, each using this layout. In other words, while this idea was in vogue, which was between about 1540 and 1570, it was used by all the Oxford binders, and was not the trademark of any one workshop.

The central point here is that the expression of individuality through the obvious channel of distinctive graphic effects — either as tool designs or decorative layouts — was no part of the bookbinding culture of the time. It was not practised by the binders and was presumably not expected or missed by the customers. Despite the fact that they were producing objects which may strike us today as satisfying in a very aesthetic way, the binders were not artist-craftsmen in any William Morris or Designer Bookbinders kind of sense. They did not want their bindings to look different from those of their competitors in trade, they wanted them to look the same. I do not believe there is any element of imitation as deceit or homage here — binder B was not trying to trick the customer into thinking that his work had really come from the superior workshop of binder A — it merely reflected contemporary expectations.

Besides the survival of the bindings themselves, do we have any primary documentary evidence which casts light on the attitude of owners to their books as physical entities? By documentary evidence I mean contemporary written sources which deal directly with the purchase and appearance of books: instructions from buyers to binders, correspondence which comments on books, or anything else of this nature. The first and most important observation about this class of

Fig.2. Three Oxford bindings, made in different workshops *c.*1545-65:

bottom: T. Trebellius, *Linguae latinae . . . promptuarium*, Basle, 1545. Magdalen College, Oxford H.10.11. Bound using Gibson rolls VIII, X. *Reproduced by permission of the President and fellows of Magdalen College.*

centre: Peter Chrysologus, *Opus homiliarum*, 1541. St John's College, Oxford D.3.4. Bound using Gibson roll XX, Oldham roll IN(2). *Reproduced by permission of the President and fellows of St John's College.*

top: W. Alley, *The poore mans librarie*, London, 1565. Corpus Christi College, Oxford Δ.11.10. *Reproduced by permission of the President and fellows of Corpus Christi College.*

material is that it is very scarce, and really we have only a few isolated examples. The best known, which has nothing to do with Oxford, is perhaps the series of notes which survive in some of Sir Robert Cotton's manuscripts, giving directions to his binders, some of which were transcribed by Colin Tite in his Panizzi lectures:

'Bind this book as strong as you can', he wrote in the book which is now Titus E.VII. 'Cut it smothe. Beat it and press it well. And put a gard of parchment brod to both the quaternio first and last to past downe to the cover. Sew it with twisted and waxed threde. Let me have it on Thursday at the furdest.'[10]

The thing which strikes me immediately about this instruction is that it is primarily concerned with the structural soundness of the finished object rather than with what it looks like. 'Bind this book as strong as you can and very fair in this read leather, shewed with 3 dooble threds' — the same emphasis on strength and the use of suitable materials is evident here, although there is also a concern about the colour of the leather, and we know that Sir Robert did regularly express interest in the colour and quality of the covering material. Some of his other surviving instructions do specify purely decorative features, such as the note in Domitian. VII to 'sett flowers of gold one the back and corners and mak it very fayre'.[11] Less well known, but also available in printed transcript, are the thoughts on bookbinding which Sir Thomas Tresham imparted to John Case in 1598; Tresham was one of the most significant early donors of books to St John's College, Oxford, and Case was a one-time fellow of the College:

'The binding up of yor Library bookes', wrote Tresham, 'is spetially to be respected for the well preseruing of them and reddier vse of them. first wheather in wad or in paste bords I preferr the past bords, if they be such dooble past bords as we receave from Paris binding. . . . Then in what leather, and whether all in one coloured leather or diuers. Likewise for coloring the leaues etc. The more diuersitye of coloures and differences, be it in the couerings, false coverings, leaffes or stringes. the better will the same serue for distinguishing between booke and booke, and withall fitt all other vses so well, as if they had alonely ben of one coloure . . .'[12]

Here again the emphasis is on practical concerns, on binding for the well preseruing and readier use of the books, with no hint that they should look nice. The apparently decorative aspects of leather colour and edge colour are regarded entirely from the point of view of usefulness, to help to tell the books apart. The approach is definitely a no-frills one, in tune with the slightly later advice of Gabriel Naudé, as translated by John Evelyn, whose *Instructions concerning erecting of a library* tell the reader 'to retrench and cut off all the superfluous expences, which many prodigally and to no purpose bestow upon the binding and ornaments of their books, and to employ it in purchasing such as they want . . . it becoming the ignorant onely to esteem a book for its cover'.[13] One other piece of primary evidence in this area that I know of is the instruction concerning the binding of one of Sir Edward Paston's late sixteenth-century music books, which survives on a flyleaf of a manuscript now in the Royal College of Music, which reads: 'I pray bynd this book in yellow lether duble fillytd wt sylver, my Mr his ovell and his name vppon it, the leaves be sprinkled wt green & greene silke stringes; look to fould it very even and cutt it as little as may be'.[14] This is less puritanical in tone, and seems to be concerned with purely aesthetic questions like the silver fillets and the centrepiece tool to be used for decoration.

The problem about this kind of evidence is that we have so little of it. What we need is contemporary documentation in the form of letters or diaries in which people express opinions about the physical qualities of the books they are buying, and this simply does not exist in meaningful quantity. I sometimes hope that somewhere, hidden in some record office or library, is a cache of undiscovered letters between two friends or colleagues of this period in which they swap comments about books they have been buying—'I've just been to binder X because I think he's better than Y', or 'because I like his new style', that kind of thing—but I have yet to discover it. There are letters like this that talk about the obtaining of specific titles, and the difficulties of getting hold of them, but the emphasis is always on texts rather than bindings.

One noticeable characteristic of the Oxford binding trade at this time which supports the view that quality was perceived primarily in terms of function is the extensive use of manuscript waste as pastedowns. As Neil Ker observed and documented, Oxford binders carried on using pieces of cut-up medieval manuscript to line the insides of their boards for longer than was the case in other English binding centres.[15] They did this routinely in the first three quarters of the sixteenth century, less regularly in the fourth quarter and occasionally in the first quarter of the seventeenth century. The recycling of waste material, both manuscript and printed, is a common feature of all English binding practice throughout the sixteenth century and well into the seventeenth, but the general trend is towards the increasing use of plain white paper as time progresses. The reasons for the change were, surely, aesthetic ones; it is more pleasing to open a book and find clean white endleaves than to find cut-up leaves from a separate and unconnected work. The introduction of marbled endleaves, which comes into English binding practice in the second quarter of the seventeenth century, is a part of this continuing trend and shows a clear interest in the use of the first opening of the book as an arena for decoration. The fact that most people today find it more *interesting* to open a sixteenth-century book and find a leaf of thirteenth-century manuscript than to find virgin paper should not corrupt our judgement. The use of waste for endleaves was undoubtedly done for economic and structural rather than decorative reasons and there was no intention to please the eye of the user by putting in manuscript pastedowns. If this was the case, we would surely detect some attempts to insert it so that the text is the right way up, or central on the page, or to ensure that pieces of the same manuscript were used front and back, but this kind of consideration never seems to have entered the binders' thinking. They cut the vellum so as to obtain as many usable pieces as possible, and regularly used scraps from different manuscripts at the two ends of their books. If there was any kind of aesthetic rebellion against this practice, we might expect to find the reaction setting in at the better end of the market, but this is not demonstrably the case. The richer colleges like All Souls and Merton, whose library funding allowed them to have extensive quantities of local binding work done in the late sixteenth and early seventeenth centuries, have rows of bindings of the 1580s and 1590s in decorated leather over wooden boards with vellum manuscript pastedowns. At All Souls in the 1580s the binder was even allowed to cut 30-odd leaves from one of the Library's thirteenth-century manuscripts to provide pastedowns for the bindings of the Antwerp polyglot.[16] The carrying out of what we might call fine binding work was much more restricted in Oxford than it was in London, but the use of gilt tooling came to Oxford in the 1560s and there was evidently some market for this from then onwards. Some of these 'luxury' bindings have plain endleaves, but many do not; Neil Ker's survey of fragments in Oxford bindings lists a number of gilt bindings of the later sixteenth century which contain manuscript waste pastedowns.[17]

The college libraries of Oxford contain many personal libraries built up by academics during the period defined in my title, which were absorbed in whole or in part after their owners' deaths. At All Souls, there are the books of Dudley Digges, who had already amassed a collection of over 1300 volumes at the time of his early death in 1643, aged only 30, although not all of those books remain in All Souls today. Brasenose also received three personal libraries in the 1640s, each several hundred volumes strong, from Henry Mason, William Hutchins, and Samuel Radcliffe. The library of Robert Burton, who died in 1640, is split between Christ Church and the Bodleian, and is well documented through the work of Nicholas Kiessling, whose catalogue of the entire collection was published in 1988.[18] At Corpus Christi, we have the books of Thomas Greneway, President of the College, who died in 1571; we also have an appreciable chunk of the library of a slightly later President, John Rainolds, who died in 1607, and the collection of 750 books given by Brian Twyne when he died in 1644. Jesus College has the books of Griffin Powell, Principal from 1613 until 1620, as well as part of the collection of Edward, Lord Herbert of Cherbury, who died in 1648. Although less than halfway through the alphabetical roll call of colleges, this is by no means a complete list; the pages of Paul Morgan's guide to *Oxford libraries outside the Bodleian* contain some of the names that could be added to the list, as well as the names from Lincoln to Worcester.[19] There is no shortage of material for study; the problem lies more in isolating the different collections and recognizing the general trends and patterns.

At this point, we might construct a working hypothesis something like this: the average working scholar in the sixteenth and seventeenth century in Oxford was likely to be a book owner and might commonly be an owner on quite a large scale, with a personal collection of perhaps several hundred volumes. His books would be acquired for textual reasons, and his interest would centre around those texts. He would wish his books to be structurally sound and serviceable, so he would prefer them to be leather-bound for durability. His bindings might be decorated, but only because it was the style of the day and the way the bookbinders naturally produced them. He would give little or no thought to the decoration of the bindings and his approach to book ownership would be very much inclined towards practicality rather than luxury.

It is not hard to find evidence to support this hypothesis. Dudley Digges's books in All Souls are more often than not in very plain early seventeenth-century bindings, with no inscription or other annotation by their owner. The same observations apply to the books of Henry Mason and William Hutchins at Brasenose. John Rainolds is another person who did not write his name in his books, although his bindings are usually decorated. This tendency not to put ownership inscriptions in one's books is noticeable among a number of other collectors, including William Paddy and Philip Bisse, each of whom gave large collections of books to St John's and Wadham respectively in the early seventeenth century. Other non-inscriptional owners include Samuel Radcliffe and Leoline Jenkins. Is this question of the extent to which people record their ownership in their books a relevant one in the context of establishing their attitude towards their books? It surely must be, in the sense that the absence of marking seems to imply a more casual attitude to ownership than the reverse. The ostentatious display of ownership through names, initials or armorials stamped on to bindings is certainly not an observable feature of the Oxford book-owning culture at this time. On the other hand, the use of mottoes or other inscriptional devices by some owners shows an inclination to use the opportunity to write on a title page as more than purely a security device. Griffin Powell's books normally include both his name and his favoured motto, 'O Jesu este mihi Jesus/Dominus mea portio' at the top of the title page. Toby Matthew's books from the 1560s and 1570s, collected while he was a graduate and canon of Christ Church, Oxford but now in York Minster Library, usually carry the motto 'Vita Christus mors lucrum'. Robert Burton, whose books are fairly scruffy and commonplace from a binding point of view, commonly wrote his personal cipher in his books, three r's representing the three letters r in his name, as well as his full name or initials.[20] How are we to interpret this kind of fancy? Is this a form of bibliophily, or of vanity? This kind of annotation seems to be using the books as vehicles for self-expression by the owners, but does not necessarily provide evidence of an interest in the books as physical objects.

I mentioned earlier that John Rainolds's books were usually decorated and this is indeed the case. Rainolds was acquiring his collection in the later decades of the sixteenth century when the standard option for a leather binding in Oxford was something in very dark brown calf decorated with a blind-stamped centrepiece and possibly a frame or frames of blind fillets, with small ornaments at the corners, depending on the size of the book. Fig.1 is a typical example. Books looking like this were produced in their thousands, and many survive today. There are lots of them on the books from Rainolds's library now in Corpus Christi, and in other college libraries, and they have no apparent distinguishing features to individualize them, among the mass of other bindings owned by Rainolds's many academic contemporaries. Much the same can be said of many other late sixteenth-century Oxford collections—Toby Matthew at Christ Church, Griffin Powell at Jesus, John Jackman at Oriel. The general characteristic of all these libraries, from a physical and decorative point of view, is that most of the books are in perfectly standard bindings of their time, decorated according to the fashion of the day and all looking much the same. One notices neither any tendency towards individual characteristics, in the way that it is possible to identify Middle Hill boards or a John Bellingham Inglis binding, nor does one detect any concern for standardization or consistency within collections. None of these men appears to have made any effort to have the same rolls or centrepieces on all their bindings. The prevailing impression is that they took what came from the vendors and did not waste too much time worrying about the external decoration.

There were however different levels of decorative quality; the market offered a range of options from the simple through to the more elaborate and there are cases where one can detect that an individual was regularly acquiring bindings from the higher end of the scale. Thomas Greneway, who was President of Corpus Christi from 1562 to 1567, left his books to the college when he died in 1571. His generosity towards the college was evidently undimmed by the fact that he resigned the Presidency after a bitter dispute with some of the fellows, who accused him of all kinds of improprieties including the allegation that he committed adultery with the wife of a bookbinder.[21] Many of his books are in handsome roll bindings of mid-brown calf over wooden boards, often quite elaborately decorated like the example shown in fig.3. To modern eyes they are certainly a cut above some of the other bindings which were being produced in Oxford at this time. Someone at the other end of the career scale in the 1560s was Philip Bisse, who graduated in 1560 and spent the rest of the decade as a college fellow, first at Brasenose and then at Magdalen. Many of the books he bought at that time are products of an alternative Oxford bindery which was making roll bindings in dark brown leather, using old rolls whose impression in the leather often looks worn and imperfect, like the example in fig.4. Is it safe to draw the inference that Greneway, the President, was deliberately patronizing a superior and presumably more expensive

Fig.3.   J. Spangenberg, *Tabulae compendiosae in Euangelia*, Louvain, 1563. Corpus Christi College, Oxford GG.8.14. Bound using Gibson rolls XVI, XVII. *Reproduced by permission of the President and fellows of Corpus Christi College.*

Fig.4. St Basil, *Opera*, Basle, 1565. Wadham College, Oxford. Bound using Gibson roll
VII. *Reproduced by permission of the Warden and fellows of Wadham College.*

craftsman, than Bisse the college fellow, because he wanted fancier bindings? We should perhaps be cautious and remember that the difference in visual appeal may not have been so great when the books were new. A clearer case of comparison may be found at Brasenose, where the books of Samuel Radcliffe, who was Master of the college from 1614 till his death in 1648, may be found intermingled on the library shelves with another benefaction of the 1640s, the books of Henry Mason, who, like Radcliffe, was an undergraduate at Brasenose in the 1590s but subsequently pursued a career outside Oxford, holding various London livings and a canonry at St Paul's before dying in Wigan just a few months before Radcliffe. Mason's books are fairly plain: there are a few gilt bindings but most of the books are blind stamped, and the decorated bindings are generally sixteenth-century ones where Mason was not the first owner. Many of his seventeenth-century books, which he acquired new, are in standard plain calf bindings of that period, decorated only with blind fillets round the border. Radcliffe's books, *en masse*, are noticeably fancier, and include a number of gilt centrepiece bindings made in Oxford in the 1620s and 1630s. It is not what could be described as top of the market work, by London or Cambridge standards, but there is a perceptible difference in quality between the two collections. Radcliffe's gilt-tooled books show that Oxford binders could clearly offer a choice and that there were customers who would go for the more expensive option. Is it right to think of Radcliffe as a bibliophile, or did he acquire these more luxuriously finished books merely because they were more appropriate to his social status as Master?

Reflection on these issues inevitably leads one to wonder just how new books were sold in Oxford at this time: how many were sold ready bound, and how many were stocked in sheets, to be bound only when a customer had expressed his wish to buy? I think there is a widespread general acceptance of the idea that the usual practice of booksellers in the handpress age was to stock some books ready bound, in plain and simple bindings, and to stock some in sheets, for binding to customer specification.[22] Quite what the balance was between these two options is harder to say. Out of the many thousands of straightforward blind-stamped bindings made and sold in Oxford during this period, decorated with rolls, centrepieces, panels or smaller ornaments, how many were bought ready bound? Most, some, or none?

I do not have a direct answer to this question but I can offer a number of observations that point towards the sale of books ready bound. John Dorne's day book, which records over 1800 transactions made across his Oxford bookseller's counter in the year 1520, includes quite a lot of information about the physical state in which the items were sold.[23] Outgoing books are sometimes noted as 'ligatus', that is, bound, sometimes specifically in parchment or leather. Many entries carry no information of this sort, but about half the list is accounted for by pamphlets and broadsheets which sold for 6d. or less, whose coverings were presumably either temporary or non-existent. There are just over 400 items described as sold either in leather, in parchment, or just 'bound', and there are 71 items sold 'in quaterniis', that is, in sheets. I can see two possible interpretations of the 400 entries which were 'ligatus': either these books were sitting on Dorne's shelves ready-bound and waiting to be taken away, or they represent transactions in which the customer came in and said, 'yes please, I'll have one of those, and I'd like you to have it bound for me in leather (or whatever)'. In the second case, the books would not be bound before purchase. Were the 71 books sold in sheets taken that way because the customers intended to have them bound to their own specification by binders who were not part of Dorne's commercial network? Or were they taken that way as a cheaper option by people who intended to use them in unbound form? The possibility of different interpretations makes it difficult to establish the true picture with confidence, but I incline to the first explanation in each case as the most plausible: that the books sold bound were ready-bound before purchase, and that the books sold in sheets were being sold that way for independent binding.

During the first half of the sixteenth century a number of panel stamps were used by Oxford binders. One particular pair of panels, decorated with warriors' heads, was in use c.1535–45 and although many hundreds of bindings must have been turned out on which these panels were employed, the vicissitudes of time have meant that only a tiny proportion survive today.[24] I know of 22 examples. Even among so small a sample, it is striking that certain texts recur—three of the 22 bindings are on the same book by Joannes Ferrarius, a legal commentary on part of the Pandects.[25] Two of these three are the same 1536 Marburg edition, one is a different 1535 Lyons edition. The classical text *De re rustica* occurs twice, again in different editions, among the sample of 22.[26] As usual, the evidence is open to various interpretations, but this seems to point to the likelihood of popular texts with a known and ready market being stocked by the booksellers ready bound in anticipation of customer demand. I have also been struck by occasional instances of dated ownership inscriptions which are observably later than the likely date of binding. There are for example a couple of books in Wadham carrying inscriptions showing they were bought by a man called Walter Bower in 1555, whose bindings both bear rolls which do not appear to have been used after 1550. We cannot prove, of course, that Bower was the first owner, but my guess is that he was, and that these books were bound up in the 1540s and waited several years to find a purchasing customer.[27]

All these observations add weight to Neil Ker's comment, 'To judge from college accounts, it seems likely that new books were as a whole bought ready bound from Oxford booksellers', and suggest that this applies to personal as well as institutional customers.[28] Such an explanation of the general set-up of the retail trade would certainly accord with the mass of evidence to suggest that individuals showed little concern for consistency among the decoration of their books.

One of the things we should remember is that the normal practice of both individuals and institutions for most of this period was to store books on shelves with edges outwards, with little opportunity to display any aspect of binding decoration. It is evident from early illustrations of bookshops that they followed this practice too; there is no sense in any of these pictures that the bound books are being displayed to show off attractive bindings as a selling point.[29] It may be that owners were more interested in the look of the leaf edges than in the decoration of the covers, and Oxford binders, like all binders of this period, regularly applied coloured dye to the edges of the leaves. In the late sixteenth century the colour was most commonly yellow, changing to red or a sprinkled red in the following century, but there was scope for variety and they could also produce green or a purpley-blue. Many of these edge colours have faded over time but when they survive in unfaded state it is clear that they could be very colourful. *En masse*, they must have been quite striking; an early visitor to Selden End in the Bodleian would be presented by a much more vivid display of colour than the predominantly brown effect that greets us today. Owners commonly inscribed the fore-edges of books with hand-written titles, for purposes of identification, and occasionally one comes across owners who took more than average trouble to ensure that this was pleasingly done. Philip

Bisse is a case in point; he regularly inscribed his fore-edges in a way which shows a clear intention to take labelling beyond the merely informative to the aesthetically satisfying (fig.5). There is a set of books in All Souls which shows that concern for uniformity could extend to edges more than it could to boards. In or about 1615 the College was given volume 2 of a 3-volume set of Sleidanus's *Commentariorum de statu . . . libri XXVI* by Thomas Brett, a one-time fellow. We can tell this from the *ex dono* inscription on the titlepage. It is now surrounded on the shelves by volumes 1 and 3, which each carry the inscription 'empt: per Colleg.', that is, bought by the College. It looks as though they went out to buy volumes 1 and 3 to complete the set after being given volume 2. The binding of volume 2 is a plain early seventeenth-century calf binding, decorated on the boards only with blind fillets, with a narrow gilt roll run round the edges of the boards and a rather unusual blue/green dye on the edge of the leaves. It is not observably an Oxford binding and I take it to be London work. Volumes 1 and 3 were uniformly bound in Oxford, in similar style to volume 2 but with the addition of a blind centrepiece. They have blind fillets round the board edges, over which a gilt roll has been superimposed, and the same distinctive blue/green edge colouring. Neither the edge colour, nor the use of gilt rolls round board edges, are standard practice in Oxford at this time and my reading of the evidence is that a special effort was made to make the edge features of volumes 1 and 3 match the existing features of volume 2. They were not concerned about the lack of uniformity about the boards – the 2 outer volumes have centrepieces while the middle one does not – but they did care about the edges, because that is what they actually saw.[30]

There is one particularly intriguing exception among this general picture of owners who accepted what came from the binders without apparently interfering in the question of decorative features, and this is to be found among the books of Brian Twyne. Twyne is well known as one of the great early antiquaries, whose manuscript collections on the history of Oxford have been extensively quarried by writers from Anthony Wood onwards. He spent most of his life in Oxford, as a graduate and fellow of Corpus Christi, as Reader in Greek, and as Keeper of the University Archives, and when he died in 1644 he bequeathed to Corpus 'all such bookes that they have not in their library'. Twyne's collection of printed books was rich and remarkable in many ways, and we only know about the part of it, albeit sizeable, that

Fig.5. The characteristic fore-edge labelling of Philip Bisse. *Reproduced by permission of the Warden and fellows of Wadham College.*

went to Corpus. It comprised the accumulations of several generations of Twynes, and besides many standard and scholarly works in theology, classics, law, medicine and the like it includes many rare and ephemeral STC items on such subjects as angling, chess, gardening and necromancy. A catalogue of Twyne's library was published by the Oxford Bibliographical Society in 1952 and this is not the place to consider its contents in more detail.[31] Nor do I intend to look at his bindings comprehensively or systematically; his library includes many typical bindings from Oxford and elsewhere made during his period of collecting, which was the first half of the seventeenth century, and he inherited sixteenth-century bindings from his father's collection. What is particularly interesting in the context of this essay is a small group of a dozen or so Oxford bindings whose decorative pattern appears to be unique to Twyne. These books are bound in vellum over boards and decorated with centrepieces applied not in the usual blind or gilt way, but using black ink or dye to produce a black on white effect which is quite striking. There are several centrepieces used in this way, all Oxford tools, and the date of binding is likely to be around 1610–20. An example is shown in fig.6. What I find particularly interesting about these books is not the black on white technique itself, which is uncommon but not unknown in English practice, although less uncommon on the continent, but the fact that only Twyne seems to have had his books bound like this. I have looked at thousands of Oxford bindings by working systematically along the shelves of most of the Oxford colleges and I have never found any bindings like this outside the Twyne books in Corpus. Oxford bindings of black-tooled vellum appear to be unique to Twyne. How did this come about? Did Twyne initiate a process of experimentation, or ask for something different? The books are mostly collections of pamphlets of wide ranging date, from the middle of the sixteenth century to the beginning of the seventeenth, and were presumably loose in Twyne's collection before he gathered them together for binding. Did the idea for black on white originate with Twyne, or with a binder? Having successfully established the technique, which produces results which are clearly visually pleasing, why were not bindings like this produced for anyone else? Distinctive bindings decorated only with non-personalized tools which can be immediately associated with a particular owner are extremely unusual in English binding practice at this time – it is hard to think of another instance –

Fig. 6. L. Gauricus, *Tractatus astrologiae*, Nuremberg, 1540, and other tracts. Corpus Christi College, Oxford Φ.A.1.8. Bound for Brian Twyne. *Reproduced by permission of the President and fellows of Corpus Christi College.*

and this does look like an early and intriguing example of pure bibliophily.

What conclusions, if any, can we draw from this extensive pool of evidence? This essay has posed more questions than it has provided answers, and many of my queries remain unsolved. There seems plentiful evidence to support the theory that Tudor and early Stuart scholars were on the whole not bibliophiles, that their interest in books was text-centred and that they gave little thought to the binding beyond requiring structural soundness. On the other hand, we can sometimes perceive a tendency towards greater luxury, of a purely aesthetic kind, in the collections of better-off individuals.

The technology of book production, which made every book a hand-finished artefact, incorporated a potential for individuality which is not available to book purchasers today. Should we be surprised that that potential was so little exploited? I believe the answer to this lies with a position set out by Hugh Trevor-Roper, at the beginning of his book about Laud, when he identified himself with those 'who believe, as an historical axiom, that human nature does not change from generation to generation except in the forms of its expression and the instruments at its disposal'.[32] The great majority of book buyers today give little or no thought to the physical characteristics of their books – they buy them for their texts, as working tools or as vehicles of entertainment, and they do not bother much about the way they are bound, if they think about it at all. They do not inscribe them and although modern book marketers make use of the potential of pictorial covers to help sell them, people buy them in anticipation of what they will find inside. Like the buyers of previous generations, today's purchasers want structural soundness – they will not buy a book if its leaves are falling out – but they do not much care beyond that. Within that general trend there is a small minority of book buyers who are also bibliophiles, who do cherish and think about their books as physical objects, who adorn them with bookplates, who acquire them as collectable artefacts, but we must remember that they are a minority. If this is the general picture today, why should it have been any different 400 years ago? This analysis may seem contentious and readers may disagree with my conclusions, and wish to debate the observations I have made. In that case this essay will have served its purpose.

References

1. S. de Ricci, *English collectors of books and manuscripts*, Cambridge, 1930, p.33. This subject has recently been considered further by Jacqueline Glomski in 'Book collecting and bookselling in the seventeenth century: notions of rarity and identification of value', *Publishing History* 39 (1996), 5-21.
2. See R. J. Fehrenbach and E. S. Leedham-Green (eds), *Private libraries in Renaissance England*, New York, 1992-, vol.2 onwards.
3. J. McConica (ed.), *The history of the University of Oxford: volume III: The collegiate university*, Oxford, 1986, p.665.
4. *Ibid.*, p.646.
5. In a copy of T. Linacre, *De emendata structura Latini sermonis*, 8vo, Basle, 1560: Jesus College, Oxford M.1.28.
6. See, for example, the portraits reproduced in R. Strong, *Tudor & Jacobean portraits*, London, 1969, plates 129 (Drake), 539 (Salisbury), 639 (Walsingham).
7. These portraits will be found reproduced as follows: Rainolds and Humfrey in McConica, *op. cit.*, plates XVIa, XVIb; James in I. Philip, *The Bodleian Library in the seventeenth and eighteenth centuries*, Oxford, 1983, plate 4; Bodley in Royal Commission on Historical Monuments (England), *An inventory of the historical monuments in the City of Oxford*, London, 1939, plate 143; Grindal in P. Collinson, *Archbishop Grindal 1519-1583*, London, 1979, plate 7.
8. Mrs R. L. Poole, *Catalogue of portraits in the possession of the University, colleges, city and county of Oxford*, Oxford, 1912-26.
9. Seven of these centrepieces are reproduced in N. R. Ker, *Fragments of medieval manuscripts used as pastedowns in Oxford bindings*, Oxford, 1954, plates VI, X.
10. Transcribed in C. G. C. Tite, *The manuscript library of Sir Robert Cotton*, London, 1994, p.46.
11. *Ibid.*, pp.48-9.
12. N. R. Ker,'Oxford college libraries in the sixteenth century', *Bodleian Library Record* 6 (1957-61), 459-515, p.515.
13. G. Naudé, tr. J. Evelyn, *Instructions concerning erecting of a library*, London, 1661, p.61.
14. P. Brett, 'Edward Paston (1550-1630): a Norfolk gentleman and his musical collection', *Transactions of the Cambridge Bibliographical Society* 4 (1964), 51-69, p.58.
15. Ker, *Pastedowns*, p.vii.
16. *Ibid.*, no.995 and p.xi.
17. *Ibid.*, nos.1385, 1584, 1585, 1852, 1923, 1963, 1949.
18. N. K. Kiessling, *The library of Robert Burton*, Oxford Bibliographical Society Publications n.s.22, Oxford, 1988.
19. P. Morgan, *Oxford libraries outside the Bodleian*, 2nd edn, Oxford, 1980.
20. An example is reproduced in Kiessling, *op. cit.*, plate II.
21. T. Fowler, *The history of Corpus Christi College*, Oxford, 1893, p.117.
22. See R. B. McKerrow, *An introduction to bibliography for literary students*, Oxford, 1927, p.123; P. Gaskell, *A new introduction to bibliography*, Oxford, 1972, p.146; G. Pollard, 'Changes in the style of bookbinding, 1550-1830', *The Library* 5th series 11 (1956), 71-94, p.76.
23. Transcribed and edited as F. Madan, 'The daily ledger of John Dorne, 1520' in

C. R. L. Fletcher (ed.), *Collectanea: first series*, Oxford Historical Society, Oxford, 1885, 71-177.

24. The panels are HM.25/HM.26 in J. B. Oldham's scheme of classification, set out in his *Blind panels of English binders*, Cambridge, 1958.

25. J. Ferrarius, *Ad titulum Pandectarum, de regulis iuris . . . commentarius*: Marburg, 1536 edition (Adams F279) at Oxford, Christ Church f.6.23 and San Marino, Huntington Library 5924; Lyons, 1535 edition at London, Lincoln's Inn Library.

26. *De re rustica*: Basle, 1539 edition (Adams G448) at Oxford, Merton College 67.d.13; Zurich, 1528 edition (Adams S808) at Cambridge, St John's College Mm.6.45.

27. Oxford, Wadham College I.28.12 and I.32.3 (both works by Martin Bucer, printed in Basle in 1547 and 1536). Another similar example is Oriel 4Z.a.4 (Plato, *Opera*, 1539), bound using a combination of rolls (V, VI, XI) not used after 1545; the inscription on the titlepage, 'Roberti Whittoni liber . . . 1548' is plausibly that of its first owner.

28. Ker, *Pastedowns*, p.205, note 3.

29. See, for example, plates 21 and 28 in S. Taubert, *Bibliopola*, Hamburg and London, 1966.

30. The books are All Souls SR.d.3-5. Volumes 1 and 3 carry Ker's centrepiece vi(a).

31. R. F. Ovenell, *Brian Twyne's library*, Oxford, 1952. Ovenell did not comment on Twyne's bindings, beyond saying that they are 'nearly all in contemporary, workman-like bindings, with a large number in a parchment style executed in Oxford and apparently favoured by Twyne' (p.6). The other main published source on Twyne is an article by Strickland Gibson, 'Brian Twyne', *Oxoniensia* 5 (1940), 94-114. This is mainly concerned with his University career and writings and (perhaps surprisingly, given the author) does not discuss Twyne's bindings.

32. H. R. Trevor-Roper, *Archbishop Laud 1573-1645*, London, 1940, p.1.

Scholar-collectors
and their bindings

MIRJAM M. FOOT

LORD ACTON, historian, close friend of Gladstone, and himself no mean book collector, has been credited with the remark that 'a scholar reads a book a day'. The scholars he had in mind were perhaps not those to whom this volume is devoted, but the connection between scholars and books is an obvious one. That between collectors and reading may be less so. To judge by the immaculate state of some finely-bound vellum or large paper copies from previous centuries, a number of the most famous collectors either did not read at all, or had 'reading' copies as well as collectibles. Much has been written about those to whom the exterior of the book provided as much as, or probably more aesthetic satisfaction than, the interior and I do not propose to discuss them or their bindings here – however tempting the fruits of their taste and the artistry of their binders may be. Instead I would like to look at some ordinary scholars' bindings, limiting these to the late fifteenth and early sixteenth centuries, and then to explore with the help of four examples the relationship between scholar-collectors and their binders.

Before the binding became an integral part of the book as offered for sale, the decision whether or not to bind a text had to be taken by the producer of the book, by the publisher, the printer, the bookseller, sometimes by the author, more usually by the purchaser. The reasons for such a decision varied from giving a frequently-used book better protection, to making the text inside appear more attractive, as a demonstration of the importance attached to the contents, or as a manifestation of the importance of the owner or the recipient. Scholars would probably act for the first and third of these reasons, authors, publishers and booksellers for the second and the fourth, while some collectors might also be influenced by the last reason. The scholar-collector would either buy his books ready-bound, unbound in sheets, or, as appears also to have been the case (at least from the early sixteenth century onwards) sewn, with endleaves, but without a cover or with only a temporary parchment wrapper. In *A Millennium of the Book*[1] Nicholas

Pickwoad showed a number of examples of what he called 'interim structures'. For owners of such books, or of books in publishers' bindings, and even for those who bought their texts in sheets and had them bound to order, the binding appears merely to have been a way to hold the sections together, to protect the text from wear and tear and to make it easy to handle and safe to use.

For some scholars the binding may have reflected the importance attached to the text it contained. In the quiet and possibly less hurried environment of the monastery, the demands of daily survival would not get in the way of the study of the word of God and of theological discussion. The documentation of such discussion, the copying of sacred texts and of the commentaries of the holy fathers, deserved time and attention, and time and attention were equally spent in protecting and sometimes adorning the manuscripts thus compiled. Medieval monastic bindings were soundly constructed, sewn with thick thread all along, fastening every gathering to each of the stout sewing supports (made of cord, alum-tawed or tanned leather, or vellum) with well-thought out, often intricate sewing patterns, using solid wooden boards through which the sewing supports were firmly laced in, and secured in holes and tunnels (in a wide variety of patterns). They have properly constructed endbands, usually sewn over cord, leather or vellum cores[2] and tied down in the centre of each gathering, while the whole book is covered with good quality leather, and fitted with metal fastenings usually on leather thongs. Manuscripts written on vellum or parchment required such solid construction, but even the manuscripts on paper, although needing different techniques to accommodate the thinner and more pliable material of the text block, were constructed with care and attention to detail, producing handsome and durable books. The monks and nuns who owned these books used them either for private devotion or for study. They were frequently religious texts, but by no means always. Nikolaus Unbehaun, a fifteenth-century Dominican friar at Bamberg (Germany), a scribe who copied texts for the monastic library there, owned a thirteenth/fourteenth-century manuscript of two legal texts, sewn on three double cords and bound in calf over beech-wood boards (the lower of which showing signs that the binding was once chained), decorated by the binder who signed himself 'Mair bb' with dog, stag, and flower-pot tools (fig.1), while the upper cover shows Unbehaun's family's coat of arms in cut leather.[3] Prior Peter Knorr of

Fig.1. A binding for Nikolaus Unbehaun by Mair bb. On: Aegidius de Fuscarariis, *Ordo iudiciarius*; Rolandinnus Passagerius, *Summa artis notariae*, ms. thirteenth/fourteenth century. Staatsbibliothek Bamberg, Msc. Can. 87 (lower cover).

Nuremberg (d.1478) studied the *Decisiones Rotae Romanae* (Rome, Han and Chardella, 1472) and had it bound in brown calf over wooden boards, also decorated with blind tools, as well as cut-leather work, resulting in his coat of arms below the initials 'ihs'.[4] Study being all but the prerogative of the clergy, inside monasteries and outside, examples of well-bound and decorated books owned by them abound. Georg von Gottsfeld, canon in Bamberg, and later senior chaplain at the court, owned at his death in 1495 a library of 75 books (described in the inventory as 'clainer und grosser': small ones and large ones[5]), the binding of one of which, on a copy of Rainerius de Pisis, *Pantheologia* (Basel, [B. Ruppel, c.1468]) supposedly depicts him sitting at his desk below his coat of arms.[6] Another canon in the same town who divided his career between church and state, was Hertnidt vom Stein (d.1491), whose copy of the *Decisiones Rotae Romanae* ([Rome], Ulrich Han, [c.1470]), a much-bound and probably much-studied text, proudly displays his coat of arms on the upper cover and individual hand tools on the lower cover.[7] Those of his bindings that have survived all come from the same shop, that of Mair bb, a binder who worked in Bamberg in the second half of the fifteenth century. They are in brown calf over wooden boards and have clasps hinging on the lower cover, three with very similarly engraved plates, while two have bosses in the shape of small five-petalled flowers. Four bindings for Hertnidt vom Stein are in the Staatsbibliothek at Bamberg and have another feature in common: the edges of the leaves have been decorated in brown with drawings of scroll work, branches and leaves on a dotted ground. One has a large crouching lion on the fore-edge and two have, also on the fore-edge, two large dragons, their necks intertwined, biting their own backs.[8] The leaf decoration on the edges is closely similar to the cut-leather work that surrounds the coat of arms on the upper covers of these bindings (fig.2).

When printing was still in its infancy, the tendency persisted to provide those books for which a binding was required with the same solid and careful construction that was so characteristic of the products of the monastic bindery. But not for long. Once multiple copies of texts could be (and were) produced more cheaply, certainly more quickly, more easily and in larger numbers, the binders felt themselves compelled to speed up production and to cut costs. In *A Millennium of the Book* Nicholas Pickwoad described in detail how the binders coped with ever larger quantities of books and how, especially during the first quarter of

Fig.2. Painted edges on: (top) *Decisiones Rotae Romanae* [Rome], Ulrich Han [c.1470]. Staatsbibliothek Bamberg, Inc.typ.F.III.7; (bottom) Laurentius de Valla, *De elegantia linguae Latinae*, Rome, J. P. de Lignamine, 1471. Staatsbibliothek Bamberg, Inc.typ.N.II.6.

the sixteenth century, cheaper structures and less time-consuming practices were developed to keep pace with this increase in book production. Thinner paper and smaller formats called for thinner thread, single supports and lighter boards, as well as for less complex sewing and lacing-in methods. Already in the fifteenth century in Italy and from the beginning of the sixteenth century elsewhere, we can observe a change to cheaper materials: pasteboard replaced wood, cheaper covering materials became more prominent and we find limp parchment used for school books, tract volumes and classical texts, as well as tanned sheep, especially for smaller formats. Ties replaced clasps, paper replaced parchment for end-leaves, and we find single thongs or cords circled round by the sewing thread. Not all thongs were laced in any more and, later in the sixteenth century, the practice of sewing more than one section at a time also speeded up the process. Endbands are no longer tied down, their cores are cut off and not laced in, or they are often lacking altogether. Those cheaply-produced bindings occur most frequently on educational, religious and legal texts in small formats. They look like mass-productions for the impecunious scholar who nevertheless wanted his much-read texts protected from wear and tear. And indeed, that is what they are. We find classical and religious texts, often heavily annotated in a contemporary hand and simply bound with a cheap structure, using cheap materials and with the covers either left plain or decorated with a few blind lines. For those who wanted more decoration, comparatively simple designs could be produced where the rectangular plane of the covers is divided by blind fillets into triangular and diamond-shaped compartments, each adorned with the impression of an engraved hand stamp.

The vast quantity of blind-tooled bindings produced in Oxford and Cambridge during the late fifteenth century and the first half of the sixteenth bears witness to a clientele of dons and students (fig.3). They contain classical and religious texts, the works of humanist scholars and law books, as well as history books and grammars. The large majority of these are in Latin. Some binders worked for the booksellers and the publishers (such as Garrett Godfrey and Nicholas Spierinck: fig.4) but many bound for individual clients, and the large number of identified binders and binders' shops in both towns (and in university towns all over Europe) and the surviving evidence of their considerable output, suggests a thriving scholarly community that wanted its texts suitably

Fig.3. An Oxford binding by the Rood and Hunt binder on: Johann Nider, *Consolatorium timorate conscientie*, Paris, Ulrich Gering, 1478. British Library, IA39102 (lower cover).

Fig.4. A binding by Nicholas Spierinck on: Publius Ovidius Naso, *Metamorphoseos libri moralizati cum pulcherrimis fabularum principalium figuris*, Paris, J. Huguetan, 1518. British Library, C.66.f.7.

bound. For the simpler, less lavishly decorated bindings, the binders probably worked to a specified price, but there are instances where we can glimpse evidence of personal involvement, and the grander the collector the clearer the evidence.

Some students and scholars hovered on the borderline of being collectors. They had taste and quite clearly the funds to clothe the books they wanted to study in aesthetically pleasing garb, enlightening the mind while gladdening the eye. Some learned men started simply, but on reaching more exalted positions became less modest in their taste (or could afford to indulge it), causing their books to be embellished with gold. William Bill can be taken as an example. He studied physics and divinity at St John's College, Cambridge, where he took his B.A. in 1532/3 and his M.A. in 1536. The college elected him a Fellow in 1535 and later he became Master of St John's (1546), a lecturer in physics and vice-chancellor of the University. While a student, Bill owned two bindings decorated in blind, one by Garrett Godfrey, the other by Nicholas Spierinck, which he may have bought ready bound. Once he had become one of the chaplains of King Edward VI, he patronized the King Edward and Queen Mary binder and several finely gold-tooled bindings made for him in this shop are known.[9]

Some students had the chance to travel abroad and to receive their education at one or more foreign universities. While abroad they acquired books and had them bound to order. The German students (and cousins) Damian Pflug and Nikolaus von Ebeleben are well-known examples of this phenomenon. Not only did they acquire nicely-bound books in Paris and Bologna, mainly classical authors in Greek and Latin, but also books in the vernacular, but Nikolaus at least remained a collector for the rest of his life. An inventory made after his death shows that he owned a library of 400 books and that the value of the binding was either as high as that of its contents or, in several instances, well above it.[10] A less well-known figure is the Swiss student-collector Ludwig zur Gilgen, a member of a patrician family from the canton of Lucerne. He first studied in Freiburg in the Breisgau and at Dôle, but then continued his studies in Paris in 1565 and at the University of Orléans two years later. While in Paris he acquired several religious and botanical books which he had bound in brown calf and decorated with his coat of arms and his name. Conveniently, he had the place and date of acquisition tooled on the lower cover (in the same way as the two German cousins had done 20 years earlier).[11] There is little doubt that he (and Pflug and Ebeleben) instructed the binder as to at least this part of the decoration, and there is a great deal of evidence, provided by the bindings themselves, that owners and collectors did specify the colours of their bindings, sometimes to reflect the subject matter of the books inside, such as Pietro Duodo, Venetian Ambassador to Paris (1594-97), who accumulated a travelling library of small-sized books, bound in differently coloured leather according to the subject of the books, and decorated to very similar designs of ovals filled with naturalistic flowers, his arms and his motto. Other collectors specified the kind of decorative motif to be used, sometimes for the same reason, for example, Sir Julius Caesar (1558-1636), Master of the Rolls, whose travelling library was bound in limp vellum, tooled in gold to reflect the kind of text inside. Books on theology and philosophy were decorated with an angel, history with a rampant lion and poetry with an olive branch.[12] Some owners would specify the style or design of the decoration, for example, the French courtier and collector, Anne de Montmorency (1493-1567) who had his bindings decorated in the same style as the interior of his house in Ecouen. Whether the latter should be considered a scholar-collector or purely a collector is a moot point. He was certainly a great patron of the arts in their many manifestations, commissioning houses and castles, collecting sculpture, paintings, ceramics, tapestries, enamels and medals, as well as books and manuscripts. However, if one looks at the remaining evidence provided by his library and by the inventories made of his property in Paris, it is clear that the texts he owned, even if they were bound in velvet or in white, black and red calf, blue and green morocco or vellum, were not only those that we would expect a soldier, courtier and statesman to own and read, but also those that a scholar with distinct personal interests would pursue. He owned reference books, atlases, military works, books on navigation and on duelling, a fair amount of history, a surprising number of books on religion, as well as literature and science.[13]

Even if a twentieth-century sceptical mind may cast doubt on the profundity of Anne de Montmorency's scholarly qualities, few would deny the scholarship of one who not only collected books and had them bound to order, but who also displayed a manifest interest in how his books were bound, and of whose interest we have documented proof – as well as the resulting bindings. Sir Robert Bruce Cotton (d.1631) and his library of outstanding manuscripts were brilliantly treated by Colin Tite in his 1993 Panizzi lectures and his importance as a collector of manuscripts, not only for his own interest but *pro bono publico*, was convincingly demonstrated.[14] Very few of Cotton's manuscripts have retained their original binding; possibly because Cotton bought some of his manuscripts unbound, possibly because he followed the prevailing fashion of his time and had them rebound, possibly because several perished or were irretrievably damaged in the fire of 1731. That he took an active interest in the binding of his books is clear from the detailed — albeit somewhat repetitive — instructions to his binders written on what is now the front (or in some cases the rear) pastedown. Who these binders were or even how many Cotton patronized is not known. Only on one occasion do we read: 'sent to mr Hil [Hal?] the Bookebinder'; on another occasion reference is made to 'he in paternoster row' when Cotton himself wrote a memorandum to instruct 'he in paternoster row to sett one arms on 4 old bokes' (there are examples in Cotton's library where his coat of arms was added to earlier bindings). He also referred to 'he in Warwick Lane [who] hath bound 7 Bookes'. In many instances we read exhortations to the binder not to trim too much off the edges of the leaves: 'cut it as litle on the head as you can'; 'Set it even at the head because it shall nott be cut'; 'cut it with car[e] for you cut the last Books to[o] much'.[15] But we also read the plea to 'cutt the Book small' or to 'cut it smo[o]th', adding 'I car[e] not for the new notts [notes]', allowing the sixteenth-century marginalia in the *Catalogus Benefactorum* of St Albans Abbey to be trimmed.[16] His best-known (and most frequently quoted) binding instruction is also the most informative. It occurs on the pastedowns of the *Liber Vitae* of Durham and asks the binder to: 'Bind this book as strong as you can [a frequently-found request]. Cut it smothe. Beat it and press it well. And put a Gard of parchment brod to both the Quaternio first and last to past downe to the cover. Sew it with Twisted and Waxed threde. Lett me have it on Thursday at the furdest'. He continued: 'Bind this book as strong as you can and very fair in the read leather/let it be shewed [sewed] withe 3 double threds waxed and when it is backed and sewed send it me and I will mark wher you shall cutt it/gett it as euen at the head as you can. . .'. After having inspected it, he gave further instructions to '[cut it] as I have marcked and [round] it not to muche in the back for fear you put som leaves so forward that the[y] may be in danger of Cutting/sett flowers of gold one the back and corners and mak it very fayre and lett me have it ready this night when [I] send about 5c in the afternoone'.[17] Cotton obviously knew what he was talking about and his instructions, down to the vellum guards and the kind of thread to be used, show a particular concern for the strength and solidity of the binding structure. On another occasion he instructed his binder to use 'A leafe of parchment befor and behind',[18] thus specifying the end-leaves. As noted above, Cotton was by no means the only owner to specify the colour of leather to be used or to indicate the kind of decoration he wanted, but most of those who did fall more easily into the category of collectors than that of scholars.

Two other scholar-collectors, one also collecting during the seventeenth century, the other during the eighteenth century, have left us with evidence of their interest in the structure, colour and decoration of their bindings: Samuel Pepys and Edward, Lord Harley. Coming from different backgrounds and occupying different positions in society, they dealt with their binders in different ways: Harley through his librarian, the learned, efficient, but sometimes also rather officious, Humfrey Wanley, while Pepys' relations with his binders and booksellers was far more personal, sometimes even a little too intimate, as on the occasion on 13 July 1668, when he 'walked to Ducke-lane, and there to the bookseller's at the Bible, whose moher [wife] yo have a mind to', presumably the same lady as referred to in the entry for 10 April: 'So to . . . Duck-lane and there kissed bookseller's wife and bought *Legend*'.[19] Samuel Pepys was much interested in the actual craft of bookbinding and his diary records several occasions on which he visited his binder to watch him at work. On 2 October 1666 he went to call on 'my new bookbinder to see my books gilding in the backs', while on 18 February 1666/7 we read: 'Up, and to my bookbinders and there mightily pleased to see some papers of the account we did give the Parliament of the expense of the Navy, sewed together; which I could not have conceived before how prettily it was done.' On 31 January 1667/8 Pepys recorded: 'I to my bookbinder's and there till late at night, binding up my second part of my Tanger accounts; and I all the while observing his working and his manner of gilding of books with great pleasure.' Through the extensive research of the late Howard Nixon who, in his catalogue of the bindings in the Pepys Library, discussed the ten main styles of spine decoration and how they reflect the chronology of Pepys's acquisitions, it is clear that Pepys himself specified the way the spines of his books were to be tooled. Pepys's Diary bears witness to his involvement in the binding of his books, as well as their tooling, when we read that on 18 December 1662 he went 'to Mr. Cade the Stacioner to direct him what to do with my two copies of Mr. Hollands books which he is to bind'. On 18 January 1664/5 Pepys recorded: 'Up, and by and by to my bookseller's and there did give thorough direction for the new binding of a great many of my old books, to make my whole study of the same binding'. On 3 February we read: 'my bill for the rebinding of some old books, to make them suit with my study, cost me 3*l* – but it will be very handsome'. He collected 'the last of my books new-bound' on 10 February . . . 'and much pleased I am now with my study, it being methinks a beautiful sight'. The spines of the books were evidently not all gilt at this stage, for on 13 August 1666 Pepys went 'to Paul's churchyard to treat with a bookbinder to come and gild the backs of all my books to make them handsome, to stand in my new presses when they come'. The Great Fire of London interrupted this agreeable pursuit, but on 28 September he noted the arrival of 'the bookbinder to gild the backs of my books'. There are many more indications of this kind, and the books themselves show that it is likely that Pepys also specified the treatment of the edges. Roughly speaking, at the beginning of his collecting career he favoured red-sprinkled edges, during the middle period he preferred marbling, and towards the end of his life he reverted to sprinkling, usually in red and brown, although there are many exceptions.

When still an eighteen-year-old undergraduate at Christ Church, Oxford, Edward, son of Robert, first Earl of Oxford, was already an inveterate buyer of books, sometimes much to the distress of his tutor, Dr William Stratford, who felt himself compelled to write to Edward's father on 19 December 1708: 'I am afraid that you will be surprised, as I was, at the bookseller's and bookbinder's bills [the bookseller's bill came to £25.15.9, while the binder's bill was for £16.3.4]. . . two-thirds of the bookseller's bill are for very trash, and I am afraid at least half of the bookbinder's is for gilding and Turkey leather'.[20] At that time the young Lord patronized Richard Sedgley of Oxford whose remaining bills from the period indeed specify a good deal of gold tooling, as well as a certain amount of red and blue Turkey leather, but also some gilt red calf and a few more modestly bound books in pasteboard, pasteboard and parchment, or pasteboard and marbled paper. All his life Edward Lord Harley remained fond of Turkey leather and of what his librarian Humfrey Wanley called 'My Lord's Marocco Leather'.[21] It is not always clear whether it was Wanley or Harley himself who gave the instructions to the binders, although on occasion we notice Harley's direct involvement in the letters he sent to his librarian. On 1 August 1717 Harley wrote: 'I have sent up the Thomas Aquinas directed to you which I desire may be bound in Red Turkey Leather by Steel'.[22] On 1 January 1722/23 in a letter to Wanley from Wimpole, Lord Harley complained: 'I did many weeks if not months ago give my directions for the binding of the Virgil & Tullies Epistles. I did say that you & Elliot should consult about the method to make the leaves of vellum lye smooth & that the work should be gone upon as soon as you two had fixed upon a method', leaving the more technical discussions to his librarian, who indeed on 9 January, 'after much Conversation [with Elliott] about the best way of getting out the Cockles risen in my Lords Virgil, & Tullies Epistles, both Printed upon Velum: I deliver'd them to him [Elliott].'

Not only were Harley's binders instructed what leather to use for which books (Turkey leather or morocco for the most important manuscripts and the more valuable printed books, sprinkled calf for the less valuable manuscripts and printed books, doe skin as an experiment), they were also given instructions as to the boards, the squares, the headbands, and – most importantly – the design. I cannot prove whether it was Harley or Wanley who specified the thickness of the boards or the size of the squares, but it is remarkable that both Mrs Steel and later Thomas Elliott and Christopher Chapman, all used thicker boards and larger squares for Harley's Turkey and morocco bindings than was common at the time. Moreover, all three used the same type of red, white and blue silk headbands, sewn double with a bead, to accommodate the extra height of the headcap (caused by the large top square). Another peculiarity is that, contrary to expectation, Steel, Elliott and Chapman left the edges of the leaves of the books bound in Turkey or morocco plain, rather than sprinkling or gilding them. Wanley discussed matters of structure with the binders. We read (in Wanley's Diary) in January 1721/2, 'Mr Elliott brought in his Proposal about Binding. . . . which not agreeing with the Method I desired him to proceed by; he rated another which I drew up, & signed the same.'

The styles in which the Harleian bindings were decorated were certainly inspired, and most probably specified, by Harley himself – although sometimes the choice of the amount of decoration was left to his librarian. On 26 November 1717 he wrote to Wanley, 'I sent you a Box by the last Higler directed for you at Dover Street there was in it . . . some MSS. to be bound. I desire they may be carefully bound, you will give directions for their being bound fine or plain as you shall see the book to deserve it, I would have them all lettered.' He followed this up with a letter on 1 December, stating 'I would have Mrs. Steel bind my Books'.[23]

Mrs Steel decorated the bindings for the more important books in two styles which she called 'Red turk fill. & side tools' or 'Red Turk. Middle Piece and Side tools'.[24] Wanley gave careful lettering instructions and his Diary is full of complaints when these instructions were not carried out; Elliott especially was at the receiving end of endless complaints about his 'vicious lettering'. On 21 May 1723 Wanley made him 'take back 5 books which are Letter'd too falsely although my Titles were accurate & plain'. Sometimes his Lordship himself was dissatisfied, as on 9 July 1723 when Wanley recorded: 'Mr Elliott having brought home the two Velum books . . . My Lord made him take both back to amend their Lettering.' It was not only Elliott who made mistakes. On 6 June 1720 Wanley noted, à propos a parcel of books received back from Chapman, 'But he having blunder'd in Titling one of them: I sent him off with it, and did neither pay him, nor give him any more Work'.

Mrs Steel's style of decoration with the 'side tools' or 'side pieces', a left-over from the Restoration cottage-roof style, had become slightly old-fashioned by 1717 and Elliott and Chapman no longer used it, but there is sufficient similarity in the way the ornaments are built up from massed small tools and in the consistent use of designs, that it seems highly likely that it was Lord Harley who specified them. An indication of how much importance was attached to this type of decoration (at least by Wanley—but he was always out to please, or to avoid the admonitions of his master), became clear in a row between Elliott and Wanley. On 29 September 1722 Wanley wrote in his diary: 'Mr Elliott the Binder brought-in only 8 of the Greek MSS. I last d[elivere]d unto him; all these without mid[d]le Pieces'. A month later, on 29 October, after Elliott had delivered another parcel of books, 'A letter [was] sent to Mr Elliott, upon Occasion of his Neglect in not putting-in Midle-pieces into the Covers of such Books as he Binds for my Lord in Marocco'. The *Codex Aureus*,[25] also bound by Elliott, shows the style with middle pieces quite clearly, but one of the manuscripts that can be identified from Elliott's bill of 29 October (the day of Wanley's letter of complaint) is bound in 'My Lords Marocco', but obviously without the required middle piece. This was the binding on which Elliott got his own back by signing it with the letters of his name hidden among the tooling on the spine[26]—an impertinence which escaped even Wanley's eagle eye. Even when they were not lacking, Wanley found reason to complain, as on 12 November 1722, that on Elliott's bindings delivered two days previously, 'the Midle-pieces of the Marocco-work are all too small'. It looks as if by this time decoration with middle pieces formed the standard style and Thomas Chapman also complied, using two slightly different types, one with concave sides, the other, slightly smaller, with pronounced fleurons at top and bottom.

Pepys and Harley were both men of taste and education, both cared for the exterior as well as for the contents of their books, and both, moreover, have left us with written evidence of this care. Such documented evidence is comparatively rare, but the books and bindings acquired by scholars and collectors over the centuries, whether they were monks, clergymen, lawyers, teachers, students, courtiers, statesmen, civil servants, aesthetes, or men (and women) of letters, speak for themselves. They reflect the trends of the time, be it the state of the book trade, or the latest fashion, a way of life, a practical need, or a personal inclination. They tell us about the spread of learning, about literacy, education, scholarship, the proliferation of certain professions, but above all, they tell us about the attitudes of men and women to the books they owned and read.

References

1. R. Myers and M. Harris (eds), *A Millennium of the Book*, Winchester and New Castle, Delaware, 1994, p.70.
2. Exceptionally, some Carolingian bindings have worked endbands without cores.
3. M. M. Foot, 'Bindings with cut-leather work', *Bulletin du bibliophile*, no.1, Paris, 1991, pp.19-41, fig.5.
4. *Ibid.*, fig.3.
5. O. Mitius, *Fränkische Lederschnitteinbände aus xv. Jahrhunderts*, Leipzig, 1909.
6. British Library, IC37028. F. A. Schmidt-Künsemüller, *Corpus der Gotischen Lederschnitteinbände aus dem Deutschen Sprachgebiet*, Stuttgart, 1980, no.164. Part 1 is in the Staatliche Bibliothek at Ansbach (Inc.61). *Ibid.*, no.22.
7. M. M. Foot, *op. cit.*, fig.6.
8. *Ibid.*, fig.7.
9. M. M. Foot, *The Henry Davis Gift, a collection of bookbindings*, vol.I, London, 1978, pp.20-2, pl.I.1.A.
10. J. Hofmann, 'Die Bibliothek des Nikolaus von Ebeleben', *Zeitschrift für Bücherfreunde*, N.F.18, Leipzig, 1926, pp.86-91.
11. M. M. Foot, 'Some bindings for foreign students in 16th-century Paris', *The Book Collector*, XXIV, no.1 (1975), pp.106-10.

12. For examples of such bindings see: A. R. A. Hobson, *French and Italian Collectors and their Bindings*, Oxford, 1953, pl.30 (Duodo); H. M. Nixon and W. A. Jackson, 'English Seventeenth-Century Travelling Libraries', *Transactions of the Cambridge Bibliographical Society*, 7 (1979), pp.294-304. (Julius Caesar).
13. M. M. Foot, ' "Un grand Duc, immortel à la posterité": some bindings for Anne de Montmorency', D. E. Rhodes (ed.), *Bookbindings and Other Bibliophily, essays in honour of Anthony Hobson*, Verona, 1994, pp.117-29.
14. C. G. C. Tite, *The Manuscript Library of Sir Robert Cotton*, London, 1994.
15. Quotes from instructions on the pastedowns or endleaves of the following manuscripts: B.L. Cotton MSS. Julius F.VI, fol.315ᵛ; Vespasianus, E.III; Julius D.II; Titus A.XV, fol.305ᵛ; Domitian I.
16. B.L. Cotton MS. Nero D.VII; *see also* Vitellius D.IX.
17. B.L. Cotton MS. Domitian A.VII; fols. 1, 84ᵛ.
18. C. G. C. Tite, ' "Lost or stolen or strayed": A survey of manuscripts formerly in the Cotton Library', *The British Library Journal*, XVIII, 2 (1992), p.125.
19. For a more detailed description of Samuel Pepys's bindings see: H. M. Nixon, *Catalogue of the Pepys Library at Magdalene College, Cambridge, vol.vi: Bindings*, Woodbridge, 1984. the '*Legend*' mentioned here is almost certainly Wynkyn de Worde's 1527 edition of [Jacobus de Voragine], *Golden Legend* (Pepys Library, no.2040).
20. H. M. Nixon, 'Harleian Bindings', *Studies in the Book Trade in honour of Graham Pollard*, Oxford, 1975, pp.153-94.
21. C. E. Wright and R. C. Wright (ed.), *The Diary of Humfrey Wanley 1715-1726*, London, 1966 (and for quotations below).
22. British Library, Loan 29/249.
23. *Ibid.*
24. British Library, Loan 29/112, Miscellanea 1r.
25. British Library, MS. Harley 2788.
26. British Library, MS. Harley 3976.

Dr Andrew Coltée Ducarel (1713-1785) pioneer of Anglo-Norman studies

ROBIN MYERS

Introduction[1]

AS A HUGUENOT immigrant with gentry relations still living in Normandy, Andrew Coltée Ducarel (1713-1785) was well placed to make an antiquarian tour of that 'fine country, situated near England, and formerly so closely allied to it . . .' which had been 'for many years almost totally neglected by our ENGLISH TRAVELLERS'.[2]

Ducarel is known to historians of the book as the first of the great Lambeth librarians to leave his mark on the organization of the archiepiscopal library. He has an equal claim to fame as a pioneer in the study of medieval architecture by the comparative method, emphasizing the importance, for dating buildings, of the distinction between rounded and pointed arches. He also put Normandy, so to speak, on the map for the late eighteenth century English traveller in his *Tour through Normandy in a letter to a friend*, 1754, and its greatly expanded version *Anglo-Norman Antiquities Considered*, 1767. Towards the end of his life John Nichols published the residue of Ducarel's Anglo-Norman research, a study of the English alien priories which depended on the great abbeys in Normandy.

Ducarel moved in a circle of gentlemen antiquaries who met and exchanged ideas and publications in the Society of Antiquaries and the Royal Society and whose handsome accounts of antiquities were frequently published at their own expense for presentation to libraries and to friends.[3] Ducarel published in this tradition but, as was also customary in the eighteenth century, the heavy cost of printing the plates in *Anglo-Norman Antiquities* was defrayed by a number of gentlemen whose name and arms were engraved at the foot of each plate.[4]

Antiquarian Influences

Ducarel was elected to the Society of Antiquaries in 1737 at the age of 24. Always a gregarious man, a great drinker of both wine and tea, he took an active part in the meetings then held at the Mitre Tavern in

Fleet Street; there, in an atmosphere of conviviality, Fellows exhibited antiquarian objects in their possession which were reported in the Society's minute book. The Society published prints of antiquities and buildings which it distributed to Fellows but did not start a journal, *Archaeologia* until 1771.[5] The Fellows who had revived an earlier defunct antiquarian society in 1717 were still active in its affairs in Ducarel's younger days and among those who influenced him was William Stukeley who taught him the importance of observing the Norman versus Gothic shape of windows;[6] Martin Folkes, wayward and monied, who was 'for many years at pains to compose a History of English coins' inspired Ducarel with the idea of specializing in collecting Anglo-Gallic coins.[7] At Antiquary meetings he encountered a fellow Huguenot, Smart Letheuillier, whose commentary on the Bayeux tapestry was posthumously published as an appendix to *Anglo-Norman Antiquities Considered*[8]. Browne Willis aroused his interest in cathedral architecture;[9] and Samuel Gale, founding Treasurer of the Society, with whom he went on antiquarian tours, taught him a methodology which he later applied to the description of Norman churches.[10] Gale was Ducarel's senior by 31 years but John Nichols, in a much-quoted account, makes the tours sound like the escapades of a pair of school-boys, with Ducarel as the guiding spirit:

It was Dr Ducarel's custom to travel incognito in August with his friend Samuel Gale Esq. attended only by Dr Ducarel's coachman and Mr Gale's footman . . . It was a rule, not to go out of their road to see any of their acquaintances. The coachman was directed to say 'it was a *job*; and that he did not know their names, but that they were civil gentlemen;' and the footman that, 'he was a friend of the coachman's, *who gave him a cast.*' They usually took up their quarters at an inn; and penetrated into the country for three or four miles round. After dinner, Mr Gale smoked his pipe, whilst Dr Ducarel took notes, which he regularly transcribed, and which after his death were purchased by Mr Gough. They constantly took with them Camden's Britannia, and a set of maps.[11]

If Ducarel was to cut a figure among his antiquary friends he had to find a niche of his own. He had for some time, he explained in the preface to *Anglo-Norman Antiquities Considered*, pondered the difference between 'the mode of architecture used by the Normans . . . and that practised by the contemporary Saxons in England . . . as my thoughts on the subject did not . . . coincide with the rules then laid down in the year 1752 I went into Normandy on purpose to view to examine such buildings of duke William as were remaining in Caen, and other places in the neighbourhood . . .'[12]

On the eve of his setting forth his friend George North pointed out that: 'The great advantage of every kind which you have for travelling into those parts, which have so strict a connexion with our English antiquity, must afford infinite satisfaction to yourself, and no small pleasure to your learned friends on your return.'[13]

His Family and Background

Ducarel was the eldest of three sons born in Paris, of Jacques Coltée Ducarel (1680-1718) a Huguenot banker and merchant, a native of Caen and of his wife, Jeanne Crommelin (1690-1723).[14] Jacques Ducarel died in March 1718, just as a fresh wave of Huguenot persecution was beginning, and his widow, without a man to protect her, was at risk of having her infant sons, and a third on the way, taken from her and put into Catholic households. Her family were international bankers and merchants with a powerful branch in the Low Countries.[15] Her third son, Adrien, was born in August 1718, and towards the end of 1719, after putting her affairs in order, she fled to the security of her Crommelinck (as the Dutch branch called themselves) relations in Amsterdam, though it meant abandoning her French property and wealth, thereby confiscate under an edict of 1698. Neither Andrew, at five, nor his younger brother, James, at nearly three, could have realized the danger; 35 years later, however, Andrew was told by English students at Caen Academy that, 'As to their religion, nobody gives *them* any Trouble about it, considering them as Strangers; but I <found> heard they had lately been very severe upon the Protestant inhabitants, whose children had been forcibly taken from them.'[16] This must surely have struck a chill however much Andrew had by then come to distance himself as a naturalized Englishman. Eleven years later, his brother James heard a similar tale:

the bigot Bishop of Bayeux was said to have obtained letters of cachet to take protestant children, chiefly girls from their parents and put them into Convents . . . true or false it has spread the alarm amongst those of that religion . . . and they have had their children hid up & down the country.[17]

The young widow did not stay long in Amsterdam; in April 1721 she came to England for a family baptism, was naturalized in December and remarried in August, 1722, her new husband being Jacques Girardot, another Huguenot Norman, a wealthy timber merchant in Greenwich.[18]

Madame Girardot died in 1723, soon after the birth of a daughter, Jeanne, leaving sons of ten, nearly eight and five, and a babe in arms.[19] The three boys were tutored at home for several years[20] and in 1728, the elder two were sent to Eton where, in 1729, Andrew lost an eye in an accident.[21] Francis Grose described him graphically but spitefully as 'a large black man, with only one eye, and that of a focus not exceeding half an inch; so that whatever he wished to see distinctly, he was obliged to put close to his nose. The verses on the Cyclops did not ill describe him: Monstrum horrendum etc'.[22] He suffered from frequent eye infections, at times so bad that he could not read and his letters had to be written for him. He has been censured for failing to acknowledge the help he received in his research and writing; but his eyesight must have affected his ability to transcribe documents in unfamiliar hands, even, at times, to read printed books unaided and may account for his making all his antiquarian tours with a companion.

He left Eton in 1731 and went up to Oxford. In 1734, when they were still undergraduates, he and his brother James were naturalized. In 1738 he moved to Trinity Hall, Cambridge to study civil law, as distinct from Common Law.[23] After he came down he and James shared chambers in the Inner Temple for three years.[24]

Meanwhile the youngest brother, Adrien, was trained as a merchant in Rotterdam, made a dynastic, mercantile marriage, had four children (the only one of the brothers to have issue) and, after a brief, prosperous career, died of smallpox at the age of twenty-seven; a rebellious letter sent to 21-year-old Andrew in Oxford shews how much he resented his elders' privileged lifestyle:

Permit me to tell you that . . . living in Oxford as agreeably as man can live, having a great deal of pleasure & living pleasantly makes you forget that I should like to do so too as much as I could, you talk to me of profit, but don't consider in the meantime the pain. Lord how different you are now from what you was when I left England . . .[25]

The elder brothers seem to have had almost the rapport of twins, their handwriting so alike that at times I have had to check address and signature to tell which was which. James took immense interest in his brother's antiquarian pursuits and was well known among his friends in the Society of Antiquaries.[26] Andrew was the most intensely English of the three brothers who, although he read and spoke French fluently, wrote it as if translating, and used words which mark him as a non-native or non-resident, whereas James, whose style of writing was jaunty, often interspersed his letters with French words and phrases, sometimes for fun. He occasionally wrote in French to his brother who always stuck to rather staid English.

On being admitted, in November 1743, as a Civilian or civil lawyer to the College of Advocates (Doctors Commons) Andrew moved into the buildings which housed about thirteen to twenty ecclesiastical lawyers — a select band who prided themselves on their superiority to the much more numerous common law barristers. The connection led, in due course, to his appointment as Commissary or legal official to the Diocese and city of Canterbury and of the royal peculiar of St Katharine's by the Tower. He leased a house in the Commons which he used to the end of his life, a regular establishment staffed by a maid, foot boy and perhaps other servants. In 1757, he told his friend, Philip Morant, the Essex historian, his medical adviser warned him that he should not expect to see the end of his Lambeth work unless he 'took air and exercise; . . . that frightened me'.[27] So he took the lease on a house near Lambeth Palace, formerly owned by the Tradescants, where he lived whenever he was not at Doctors Commons.[28]

In 1749 he married his Greenwich housekeeper, Sarah Desborough, out of gratitude (according to Nichols) for her having nursed him through an illness — he was 36, she a widow of 53.[29] It was a happy if singular marriage, lasting 36 years. Perhaps she was a mother figure to a man who had scarcely known a mother. So dependent was he on her that when, at the age of 68 she fell off a ladder which she had put on a table in her garden to 'bag' some grapes, he was, as he wrote to Morant, on 13 October 1764 'almost distracted . . . she had the misfortune to fall backwards about 14 feet with her legs through the ladder — she was thereby terribly bruised but, thank God, broke no bones — she is . . . now able to crawl about & is, 'tis hoped, in no danger, so that at present I begin to recover my spirits.' James, from France, sympathized drily: 'I desire my compliments to your wife, and that for the future she would leave off riding on ladders.'

The charming message from Angel Carmey, coin dealer and FSA, described by Nichols as 'a foreigner long settled here', typifies the affectionate attitude of the Doctor's antiquary friends to Mrs Ducarel: 'The trifle of brass candlesticks I sent you yesterday,' he wrote in 1761, '. . . I wish you joy and health in wearing them with Mrs Ducarel on whom my best compliments wait'.[30]

She outlived her husband by six years, but when his nephew 'Gusty' visited her at the very end he found 'the old lady at Lambeth still living but with hardly any Faculties left so that her existence may be rather compared to vegetable than Animal life.'[31] She died, aged 95 in 1791.

The Tour of 1752

On the morning of 12 July 1752, at the start of the law vacation, accompanied by a friend (Thomas Bever)[32] Ducarel set off from Doctors Commons for the country of his birth which he had left at the age of five and now, at 39 proudly returned as a naturalized Englishman, advocate and antiquary. They avoided the fashionable route to Paris (their final destination) 'by Brighthelmstone (Brighton) to Dieppe and chose the Dover road.[33] They stayed in Dover overnight and next morning saw the fortifications and sights of the town before sailing for Calais where they disembarked on the morning of 14 July (not yet a significant date).[34] Ducarel planned a route through Boulogne, Montreuil, Eu, Dieppe, and Toste to Rouen, taking in small places on the way and examining the sights as they went across Lower Normandy to the château at Muids which belonged to his uncle, M. Crommelin de Villette, where they were 'entertained with the utmost civility by Monsieur De Villette'. This was the property which his brother James was to acquire in 1771 and Ducarel's description has a special distinction although he conceals the family connection in his published work. It was:

pleasantly situated upon a rising ground on the north side of the river SEINE, and commands a fine prospect, having two long avenues of trees running down to the river; adjoining the house, which is conveniently and elegantly built, are good offices, pleasant gardens, and a little paddock planted with trees in form of an etoille [sic]. The country about is very pleasant, affording many very delightful views to which the SEINE greatly contributes; it is chiefly a corn and hay country, there being but few vines to be seen thereabouts, but in lieu of them several fair orchards.[35]

On 23 July they spent a day in Gaillon, about two leagues from Muids where they saw the Archbishop of Rouen's palace and the nearby Carthusian monastery, 'a famous Chartreuse'. Andrew's brother James went there twelve years later two nights before the church, sacristy and chapter house, kitchen, etc., were 'reduced to ashes . . . and 4 men lost their lives or limbs in cutting off the communication of the fire to the Grand Dormitory by pulling down some building, had it reached the Cloister and Dormitory it would have spread every way and not a cell had been left . . . As there is a high hill between Muids & that Chartreuse we saw nothing of it and indeed we were all in bed.'[36]

After a week at Muids, Ducarel and Bever retraced their steps to Rouen, then doubled back to Caen for three days of intense sightseeing of the castle and two abbeys of St Etienne, *l'abbaye aux hommes*, and of la Trinité, *l'abbaye aux femmes*, founded by the Conqueror and his queen respectively; but in looking round St Etienne 'by a most unaccountable forgetfulness we omitted seeing the Conqueror's kitching'. This was a pity because it was pulled down a few years later. They visited the Caen Academy, founded, like Eton, by Henry VI, to which the English and Irish sent their sons, and 'we were very elegantly entertained by three young gentlemen students there, who shew'ed us the utmost civilities', but the accommodation was: 'Nothing more than a large boarding house,' the Doctor, partisan and scornful, commented, 'its best apartments but very indifferent and much inferior to any at Eaton.' They went to Bayeux expressly to see 'the famous tapestry . . . which was kept lock'd up in a large wainscot press in a chapel on the South side of the cathedral', the monks having no idea that it depicted the Battle of Hastings.[37] '. . . j'ay eté expres a Bayeux pour y voir les Tappisseries de Guillaume le Bastard Roy d'Angleterre, ou toute cette histoire est fort bien representée & expliquée;' Ducarel told his cousin Lieutenant Colonel Courtin (of the Regiment de Perigord at Calais) to whom he wrote 13 May 1756, '& je vous assure que je crois que cette bande de Tappisseries a Bayeux est la plus ancienne de l'Europe'.[38]

On 1 August they headed for Paris where, armed with letters of introduction from George North and Dr Stukeley, Ducarel 'waited upon' M. Claude Gros de Boze, the elderly (he died the next year) and illustrious Keeper of the French king's medals. Ducarel's published account[39] makes it sound like a meeting of minds, but a letter of January 1753 makes it clear that De Boze was less than cordial. 'Malgré la reception que M. de Boze m'avoit fait,' Ducarel wrote to a Crommelin cousin, he decided to send a 'lettre de civilité'[40] in order to secure the promised set (one of only three taken) of the 45 plates engraven of 527 coins 'from . . . the [French] King's cabinet'.[41]

Publication of the Tour through Normandy

Ducarel had kept a travel diary which it was his intention to have fair copied and circulated among his antiquary friends. On his return to London at the end of August, he set to work to polish it and turn it into a kind of guide book to Normandy. He concludes with general observations on the countryside, towns, customs and architecture. He takes special note of the shape of the doors and windows of ecclesiastical buildings, whether they were round or arched, plain or ornamented, and compares them with early churches in England, specifying Tikencote in Rutland and Iffley in Oxfordshire, their ornamentation 'differing very much from everything I saw in Normandy'. He is wrong in believing them to be Saxon but this does not invalidate his method of dating by comparison, something new in the study of architectural history.

Publication was endlessly delayed while Ducarel waited in vain for the drawings, which he had commissioned in Caen, to arrive (the author not being, as he put it 'well skilled in drawing'). The text was completed on 28 January 1753 and the 'first rough draught' fair copied and sent to George North for his comments on 9 October 1753;[42] so that when Francis Wise, Radcliffe Librarian and Oxford antiquary[43] chid him for starting work on a history of Croydon for Archbishop Herring before finishing the *Tour* Ducarel defended himself with asperity: 'I am, I assure you, neither desultory nor inconstant. My account of Normandy is long since finished, and ready for the press. I have not made the least alteration to it this great while, and have been now considerably above a year waiting for drawings from Caen: I have had several letters from thence, that they were not finished, but would soon be sent me. I have wrote over and over, and have always the same answer . . .'.[44] In the meanwhile he got cold feet—anxiously he read it over to his old schoolfellow, the Cambridge antiquary, William Cole, and sought advice, in a stream of letters, from the ever-patient Morant. Finally he plucked up courage and was 'in good earnest of thinking of printing my Tour through Normandy'. At last proofs arrived and were sent down to Morant in Colchester sheet by sheet as they came off the press. Morant covered them with extremely banal amendments. Ducarel, even though he was getting more and more nervous, ignored all of them and did well to do so: 'To tell you the truth,' he wrote to Morant, on 8 August, 'I am almost afraid to print and *am very diffident of my own performance* tho' I do not put my name to it.' and on the 24th, 'I daresay it is full of faults as to the stile, but as it is a letter to a friend, I hope it will be excused, the more readily, as all the actions there mentioned, are *true*'.

At the end of September the mountain ceased its labour and gave forth the mouse of a slim, 39-page small quarto, without illustrations, in wrappers, carefully entered at Stationers' Hall. The opening and closing

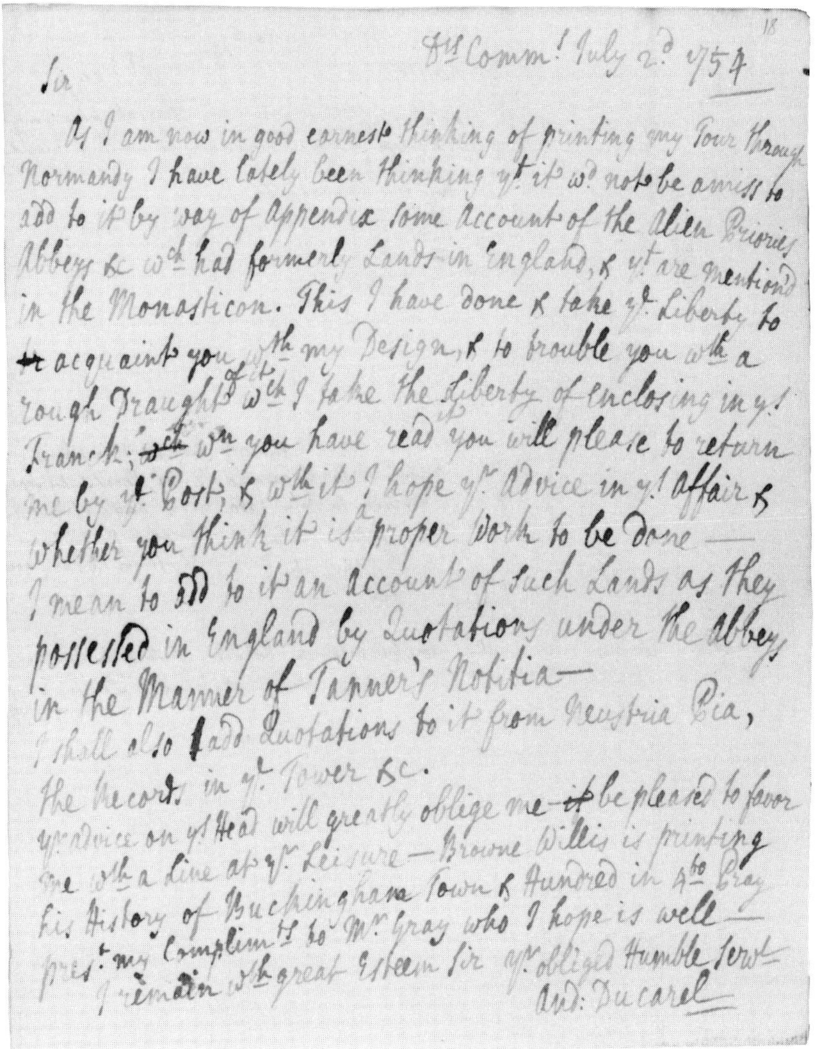

Fig.1. Letter from Ducarel to Morant, dated 21 September 1754, referring to publication of the *Tour through Normandy*. British Library, Add. MS. 37, 219, f.18.

Fig.2. Ducarel's book plate. (*Reproduced by courtesy of Brian North Lee.*)

paragraphs are addressed to George North, who, though he is not named, is the 'friend' of the *Tour through Normandy described in a letter to a friend*:

I have now, Sir, nothing to add to these observations, [Ducarel wrote in conclusion], except my good wishes, that some learned and judicious antiquary, well skilled in drawing, would take the same Tour, and rectify the errors and mistakes I have committed. I am, Sir, etc. . . . London Jan. 28th, 1753.[45]

The Doctor presented a copy to the Society of Antiquaries, another to William Derham, the President of his old Oxford college, and some dozen or score to antiquary or family friends.[46] One letter which must have been music to his ears nervously tuned for brickbats thanked him as he might have hoped:

I am doubly obliged to you, both for the Book of your Travels & the Barrel of Oysters . . . I read the Book over twice and like it extremely not only for the manner & matter of it but also on account of its being yours. The discovery you have made as to the form of the ancient windows will I question not give great light into Antiquity & for the reason you give will be always looked upon as a standing Truth by Antiquaries. The Oysters were excellent . . .[47]

Anglo-Gallic Coins

To the eighteenth-century antiquary coins and commemorative medals, being datable small objects, easily engraved and exchanged, were essential tools in the study of history; coin collecting was a fashionable pursuit and every gentleman's library contained its cabinet of curiosities, coins and medals. In collecting anglo-aquitain coins, as in that of architectural study, Ducarel's family connections gave him the advantage over native born English numismatists, whose interests were, in any case, largely in Roman coins or, if English, those minted in gold or silver.

After Martin Folkes's death in June 1754, the Society decided to engrave at its own expense 'his drawings of coins from William the Conqueror to the present time' and Ducarel was on the publications committee. This gave him the idea for a sequel; Folkes 'did not meddle with the Norman & Aquitaine', as Ducarel told Morant, so 'my account will be a sort of supplement to his work to be printed same size.' Thus was born *A series of above two hundred Anglo-Gallic or Norman and Aquitain coins . . . exhibited in twelve letters*, 1757. It is addressed to 'the Gentlemen of the Society of Antiquaries,' whose meetings and discussions led to the preservation of 'many drawings of very valuable remains of antiquities . . . [which] are happily preserved to posterity by being engraved at the expense of the society of antiquaries.'[48] It describes and illustrates 'the anglo-gallic coins struck in France from the time of William the Norman to that of King Henry VII' and its plates of engravings are enhanced by twenty-four coins taken from the French King's cabinet through the generosity of M. de Boze, Keeper of the King's Medals, who had spent many years collecting coins of 'archbishops, bishops, priors, dukes, earls etc of the different provinces of France who formerly had the right of striking coins within their jurisdictions.'[49] The 'letters' or sections of the book, spanning July 1755 to April 1757 shew that composition was, as with the *Tour through Normandy*, though for another reason, protracted. No doubt it was difficult to organize the engraving of fifteen plates of 209 coins belonging to 21 gentlemen, one lady (Mrs Amy Hasleden), four libraries and engravings made from six books in the author's own collection. By September 1754 he had 'near finished a catalogue of thirty-five Anglo-Gallic coins hitherto unpublished . . .'; by May 1755 he was 'polishing my Anglo-Gallic coins'. At the end of June he told Morant, 'the account is nearly finished. Would you give me leave to send it you down at different times, to peruse & correct before it went to press'. Then, in September he was in a quandary how to describe the crosses on coins 'in the heraldic manner'. Morant, ever generous with help and expertise, described them for him as well as contributing a 'letter' dated 11 October 1756.[50] In gratitude, Ducarel 'begged his acceptance' of a set of ten plates containing 118 coins.

Taking heart from the reception of the *Tour through Normandy*, Ducarel abandoned anonymity and put his name on the title page of *Anglo-Gallic Coins*; he went farther and put as frontispiece an engraving of himself (fig.3).[51]

Work for the Admiralty 1756-63
An illustrated reprint which would give the *Tour through Normandy* more consequence to the 'curious & learned world', had to be shelved for some years. Legal work and his duties as Lambeth Librarian, including research for books which his employer, the Archbishop of Canterbury, ordered him to produce made a return to Normandy out of the question. The outbreak of the Seven Years' War in 1756, though lines of communication were not entirely cut, made it difficult for an Englishman to go to France, although the flow of letters to and from his uncles, cousins and agents continued unabated. His brother James

Fig.3. Dr Andrew Ducarel. Frontispiece to *Anglo-Gallic Coins*, 1757.

managed to move to France in 1761 in the middle of the war and sent long, entertaining letters full of architectural information, personal gossip and commentary on the deteriorating state of France, indicating that revolution was already ominously in the wind.

Ducarel considered quitting the law for the security of a church living but circumstances were against it; the war sent his legal career in a new, more lucrative direction:

Whilst the world is distracted with wars & rumours of war etc, [he wrote to Morant on 31 July 1756], I return my daily thanks to Providence who has placed me in such a situation as to be an advocate of the High Court of Admiralty & thereby serviceable to my fellow subjects in the prizes daily taken from the common enemy & it is that which obliges me not to attempt to stir (No not for one day except Sundays) from my House; & prevents my accepting of your very kind Invitation to Colchester—where I would otherwise have gone with the greatest pleasure imaginable—having given my honour not to go out of Town at all this summer & to attend that service entirely—which is & must consequentially be advantageous to me from the perquisites arising from such attendance.[52]

Thus personal gain as much as patriotism kept Ducarel's nose to the Admiralty grindstone and we may doubt whether the prize ships would have made him welcome to the authorities in France.

The Doctor as Collector of French Books

Ducarel looked forward to meeting his cousin Milsonneau—a kindred spirit—in Paris in August 1752:

Apres avoir vu Caen & Baieux je viendray directement a Paris et d'abord que j'y seray arrivé je viendray avec un plaisir infini vous y rendre mes respects— j'apporteray avec mois le 2n Catalogue d'Osborne[53] et peutetre[54] quelque chose qui pourra vous fait plaisir—a regard des livres dont je fait mention je les acheteray moy meme a Paris; nous aurons alors le tems de parler de livres, medailles etc a loisir.[55]

Ducarel's library was a working collection. He was not concerned with fine copies, whether French or English, to judge from those of his books not uncommonly to be found in libraries, which bear one or other of his various bookplates, and from the description of the 1496 lots in Leigh and Sotheby's auction catalogue of his library, 3-10 April 1786.[56] We cannot be certain how far it represents his entire library or whether, indeed, all the books are his; but they are, in the main, just what you would expect; those on Norman or French history and the numismatic

books in French tally with many on James's lists of what he bought and
sent over to his brother in London in the 1760s, with difficulty and at
some expense.[57] The numismatic books satisfactorily match those
described in *Anglo-Gallic Coins* (predictably he had none on Greek or
Roman coins). He made much use of Bernard de Montfaucon,
Monumens de la Monarchie Francoise, 5 vols., 1729-33, in the *Tour
through Normandy* and even more in *Anglo-Norman Antiquities*. Whether
or not he acquired his copy (lot 1661 in the sale of his library) in France
in 1752, it is not in my power to say. He knew of the translation but did
not use it and may not have owned a copy as none appears in the
catalogue.[58] He had a bookhunter's ardour when he needed a book and
put Crommelin cousins to scouting for books for him both before and
after he went to France, in Paris he 'diligently enquired after a book,
entitled *Les Figures des Monnoyes de France*, in quarto, 1619, published
by John Baptist Haultin, who did not however put his name to it . . .
And it is now grown so extremely scarce in France that I almost
despaired of getting it. However I at last had the good fortune to receive
a fine copy of it from Paris. And what greatly increases its value, is the
addition of many MSS. notes, which as I am informed, are taken from
a copy of Haultin in the French king's library . . .'[59] (lot 1447 in the
sale catalogue). It was De Boze's copy. When the Keeper of the King's
medals died in 1753, Ducarel wasted no time in asking his cousin
Crommelin to acquire some of the plums of his fine library which he
had noted in De Boze's published catalogue of 1745: 'Quand la vente de
la Biblioteque de M. de Boze se fera vous noublieray pas, j'espere, mes
commissions,' he wrote on 24 January 1754, 'mais j'espere que si vous
vous porter bien j'auray bientot de vos cheres Nouvelles – j'ay l'honneur
detre avec estime . . .'.[60] But his copy of Ridolfino Venuti, *Sur les
Anciens Monumens de Bordeaux*, 1754 (lot 999 in the sale catalogue)
cannot have come from De Boze's sale because Ducarel received it from
Bordeaux 'just as I had finished the sixth plate' (of *Anglo-Gallic
Coins*).[61]

James went book-hunting for him in Caen and elsewhere.[62] 'I have
spoke to my bookseller,' he wrote from Gonneville near Caen, 15
December 1763, 'where I am retired to spend a few days of restfulness
. . . he says there are very few historys [*sic*] or books about Normandy,
that the Benedictines are at this time making a voluminous book of that
province which will contain at least seven volumes in Folio but which he
will get me a sight of when it is published in the meantime he will

introduce me to the library of a very curious gentleman in Town who has every book ever yet published relative to Normandy who is expected to come from his Seat in the country in a very few days. However I do not write this in answer to yr commissions.'

As good as his word, on 2 February, James wrote: 'the list of the Norman authors is communicated to me by Mr. Durville, those marked + I have got . . . Do not loose [it as] I have no copy—he is a gouty man, his library at his Country Seat pretty far distant. I might have trouble to get it again.'

By 1 February 1764 he had collected some 20 works, including general histories of Normandy and others on Caen, Rouen and Bayeux and their cathedrals. The list included Pierre Daniel Huet, *Les Origines de la Ville de Caen*, both the three-volume edition, 1702, and one volume of 1706 (lots 1133 and 1134). Ducarel had used a copy in the *Tour through Normandy*. His collection of French books (I have identified some 160 works, many of them sixteenth-century) must have been remarkable for an Englishman and not inconsiderable, if the Caen bookseller is to be believed, even in France.

He left his books, coins and collections to his nephew Gusty who promptly put them into auction. John Nichols and Richard Gough bought most of the papers and manuscripts.

Fashion of Windows
Ducarel recommended the *Tour through Normandy* to his cousin Courtin for the comparison of Saxon and Norman architecture:

Je vois bien que vous entendez l'Anglais . . . vous me faites, Monsieur, beaucoup d'honneur de vous donner la peine de traduire mon ouvrage—Une de mes vues principales a eté de tacher de decouvrir la differance entre l'architecture des anciens <norm> Saxons & celle des Normans—aussi bien que d'examiner les monuments en Normandie qui regardent l'histoire d'Angleterre . . . .[63]

In March 1757, he sent a copy of the *Tour through Normandy* to the Rev. James Bentham, then at work on his History of Ely Cathedral and interested in the comparison with English architecture:

Your observations there confirm the opinion I had entertained of the antiquity of circular arches, [Bentham wrote back],[64] which prevailed in this Kingdom under the *Saxon* & I think, under the first four *Norman Kings*; but in the following reign of *Hen 2* they began to deviate a little from the circular & were a little pointed; & from that time the circular came into disuse, & pointed Arches generally prevailed.

Ducarel's theory that the chronology of Saxon and Norman, or Norman and Gothic building could be established by the shape of windows was reinforced when, in the early 1760s, he was lent one of the several manuscript copies which were circulating in antiquary circles, of a section of John Aubrey's *Chronologica Architectonica* (which came to be known as *Fashion of Windows*).[65] It included rough drawings of ancient windows with some annotations and was recognized by John Britton in the nineteenth century as 'the earliest attempt at a classified arrangement of the forms of ecclesiastical windows, and therefore deserving of attention'. Ducarel and his friends got wildly excited about it and were all set to publish when they learnt that the copyright was in dispute. Short and incomplete though it was, it says all.[66]

Normandy revisited: Anglo-Norman Antiquities Considered, 1767
On 15 August 1764, when revision of the *Tour through Normandy* was well in hand, James with sibling frankness made a suggestion calculated to throw a spanner in the works:

I shall desire a learned friend of mine to put down in writing the account of some conversations he & I have had together to prove to you that there never was that distinct species of architecture which you apprehend & endeavour to prove & which is no other than the ancient gothick – I well know how unsavoury it is to any author to combat his opinion but as what I mean to procure to you will be in your own hands only & that before the second publication of your book it is not amiss that you should know what there is to be offered against it & I hope you will not be offended at it. You are in search of a truth & must hear what is to be said against your opinion and even may prick out your objections themselves somewhat material if they be found inadequate.[67]

The Doctor apparently ignored the whole thing.
The evidence of dates, headings of letters and so forth, shews that Ducarel never returned to Normandy, yet *Anglo-Norman Antiquities Considered* contains additions to the text which could not have been made from a distance and drawings which must have been procured on the spot. James's letters provide the clue – the Doctor did not have to stir an inch; in his brother James he had a deputy eager to do the legwork, revisit sights and commission drawings from M. Noel, engineer to the city of Caen, who undertook private commissions in his spare time. James concentrated on Caen but also went to Rouen, Coutances, Jumièges and gave a detailed description of the second family château of Bonnemare, once a royal hunting lodge. The Doctor had failed to get

inside the old Guard Chamber of St Etienne where the 'arms of all the noblemen who attended the Prince in his Conquest were thought to be depicted'.[68] James describes it in a lively letter, 25 January 1764: 'Yesterday' wrote James, 'I went to examine with a curious & learned antiquary the Guard Room & Baron's Hall . . . which for 300 years passed [sic] has been changed to a grainary [sic] for wheat and had the good luck to find it quite empty . . . and clean swept in order to recieve [sic] new wheat as this day — consequently I could see those coats of arms of Norman nobility you have often asked after and which few of the people even of the monks have ever heard of . . .'. Andrew reproduced the description in a watered-down version in *Anglo-Norman Antiquities*.[69] A pictorial record of the arms of the Conqueror's retinue would have greatly added to our knowledge, but presumably the guard room was filled up again before James could have got Noel to make a drawing of them.

The Conqueror's kitchen, so-called, 'with its 4 chimneys of very curious architecture' at St Etienne 'is now pulled down,' wrote Ducarel who, 'by a most unaccountable forgetfulness' had not seen it on his tour in 1752, 'but I have given a print of it, engraved from an original drawing taken by Monsieur Noel, an ingenious architect of Caen, a short time before its demolition.'[70] Through the Ducarels' good offices, the tiles from the kitchen were bought by Horace Walpole who wrote to a friend: 'I weep for the ruined kitchen, but enjoy the tiles.'[71]

James tried to find 'whether they have preserved any drawings of the many ancient fabricks which they have pulled down without interruption for these 60 years passed but they are too incurious for such ideas'. He was indefatigable in procuring drawings which would be useful for the new book: the drawing of 'St Thomas L'abbatu answers your purpose as to Norman arches, which were unknown or at least unnoticed in this town till I took hold of this church . . .'. He also sent a drawing of the east end of St Etienne 'taken from the garden. I have been, I daresay, 5 or 6 times to examine it & have carried with me not only the engineer who takes these plans for me but some of the most learned & eminent Benedictines for I am as familiar in their House as if I were founders kin . . . I believe it must please you . . . I can procure others — but I was willing to see what these would cost not to put you to an needless or great expence.'

James writes freqently of the elusiveness of Noel, who, 'I have pursued very often. He begins things for me & is called off so that I can get nothing out his hands'.[72] On 24 December 1764, 'Noel is so clever & has so much business that it is almost a peice of conjuration to hold him when one has him.' In February 1765, 'I cannot obtain Noel whilst I am absent to work on the remaining drawings he has in hand for yourself. He has so much business at all times & especially in the time of plantations & the french are so fond of a design in all that they do, that they cannot stick in half a dozen forest trees in a grass field without employing such a man as Noel to make a plan for them which must look pretty upon paper whatever it may prove in execution. This gives him so many avocations exclusive of his business for Royal Works or the Town that when he knows me absent from Caen he only gives me fair words.' He advised that, 'the west end of the Abby church of St Stephens at Caen is in my opinion not worth the drawing, however, if yr next you continue determined to have it I shall order it.' It seems that Andrew did want it probably to support his theory that the west end of French churches which 'has often round arches and no ornaments . . . induced me to think that it was often the oldest part of the fabrick.'[73] James ordered it in August having warned his brother on 18 July 1764 that: 'Noel is very busy about other matters that you must have before you can publish your book so do not hurry.'

Nichols calls *Anglo-Norman Antiquities Considered* a revision of the *Tour through Normandy* but it is, with James's additions and a good deal of new historical background, virtually a new work. He gives more detailed comparison of round arches in Normandy and England; Plate xiii shews drawings of round arches in the parish churches of Tikencote, Rutland and Iffley, Oxfordshire, the priory church of St Leonard near Stainford, Lincolnshire and the ruins of Reading Abbey which he sets beside those in the two abbeys at Caen. The text is increased from the 39 quarto pages of the *Tour through Normandy* to 176 folio pages. The plates are magnificent and the two appendixes an important addition. The Bayeux appendix is now regarded as the earliest recognition of the tapestry's connection with the Conqueror;[74] but Horace Walpole, who did not like Ducarel and was contemptuous of the Society of Antiquaries, though a Fellow, commented: 'Ducarel's book is in truth very superficial; but then the tapestry is too barbarous to impress one of anything but the ignorance and incapacity of those that made it'.[75] He added for good measure: 'The Doctor has been so bad an antiquarian himself as to insert a print of William the Conqueror dressed in the habit of Francis I'.[76]

A second appendix comprises Montfaucon's plates of a series of bas-reliefs at Rouen of the Field of the Cloth of Gold with a list of 'all those trains which actually did attend . . . the interview between Henry VIII and Francis I'. It was 'faithfully transcribed' from a contemporary manuscript which turned up in Lambeth Library when the book was already in the press and decided Ducarel on going to the extra expense of printing the Montfaucon plates.

Alien Priories

In July 1754, when the *Tour through Normandy* was about to go to press, Ducarel got the idea, apparently out of the blue, that: 'it would not be amiss to add to it by way of appendix some account of the alien priories Abbeys etc which had formerly lands in England . . . your advice on that head,' he wrote to Morant, 'will greatly oblige me.' Six weeks later he found that: 'I can't finish the abbies till I have searched the Remembran-cers Office, whose officer is out of town and when he will return is uncertain; these abbies, therefore, will, I hope, hereafter appear by themselves.' 25 years went by; no doubt Ducarel, as the Archbishop's long-standing librarian, had easier access to the documents by then. It was not until 1778 that *Some Account of the Alien Priories and such lands as they are known to have possessed in England and Wales*, for so long projected, was issued anonymously, in two small octavo volumes, printed, published, and edited by John Nichols.[77] There is some mystery about the extent of Ducarel's authorship; Nichols, in his preface, refers to 'a Gentleman whose name I am not permitted to mention, [whose] collections . . . have since been considerably augmented by some other learned friends.' This was the eccentric Somerset Herald, Thomas Warburton, who perhaps provided the text on the English priories in Volume II. Ducarel must have been, at the least, a co-author; the descriptions of priories in Normandy in Volume I are taken from *Anglo-Norman Antiquities Considered*, and the plates of both volumes are engraved by B. T. Pouncy, who succeeded Perry as Ducarel's special engraver and was his deputy at Lambeth. Some, though the artist's name is not given, may have been engraved from Noel's drawings of the 1760s; they include the west end of St Stephen's Caen with its round arches. This modest pair of volumes, whatever the truth about the authorship, is now considered the first 'modern' work on the subject.[78]

In France, *Anglo-Norman Antiquities Considered* (it was translated into French in 1823) has long been considered a key work in the rise of

French medieval scholarship in the nineteenth century.[79] On this side of the Channel, the recent interest in Anglo-Norman studies has meant that Ducarel is at last being recognized as the first English writer to compare the architecture in Normandy with that in England.

Appendix

DUCAREL'S ANGLO-NORMAN WORKS

A tour through Normandy, described in a letter to a friend. London: printed for John Woodyer, 1754. Entered at Stationers' Hall.

A series of above two hundred Anglo-Gallic, or Norman and Aquitain coins of the antient Kings of England; exhibited in sixteen copper-plates, and illustrated in twelve letters, addressed to the Society of Antiquaries of London . . . to which is added, a map of the antient dominions of the kings of England in France, London: printed for the author; and sold by E. Withers, and J. Scott, 1757.

Anglo-Norman Antiquities considered, in a tour through part of Normandy. Illustrated with twenty-seven copper-plates, London: printed for the author, by T. Spilsbury, 1767. And sold by S. Baker and G. Leigh; P. Vaillant: T. Payne; W. Owen; and J. Rivington.

[anon] *Some account of the alien priories and of such lands as they are known to have possessed in England and Wales*, 2 vols. printed and published by John Nichols, 1778.

The history of the royal abbey of Bec, near Rouen in Normandy by Dom. John Bourget, Benedictine monk of the Congregation of St. Maur . . . and Fellow of the Society of Antiquaries, translated from the French [by A. C. Ducarel], John Nichols, 1779.

CORRESPONDENCE AND PAPERS:
PRINCIPAL MANUSCRIPT SOURCES

Bodleian Library, Oxford, Department of Western manuscripts (Gough and Nichols collections)

British Library, manuscript collections

Squire de Lisle, (private collection, microfilm of correspondence in Lambeth Palace Library)

Gloucestershire Record Office

Lambeth Palace Library

Norwich Record Office

SELECT PUBLISHED SOURCES

Literary anecdotes of the eighteenth century, 9 vols, and *Illustrations of literature* . . . 8 vols. John Nichols

Horace Walpole, Correspondence, ed. W.S.Lewis, 48 vols, 1937-83

A catalogue of the very valuable library of books, manuscripts and prints of the late Andrew Coltée Ducarel . . . sold by auction, by Leigh and Sotheby, booksellers . . . 3 April 1786 & seven following days.

References

1. **Acknowledgements**. Among those to whom I am particularly indebted are Arnold Hunt, Brian North Lee, the Squire de Lisle, Giles Mandelbrote, Alison Shell, David Stoker, Jean Tsushima, Melanie Barber and Christina Mackwell and the staff of Lambeth Palace Library, and Gloucestershire Record Office.
2. *Anglo-Norman Antiquities Considered in a Tour through Part of Normandy*, 1767, p.ix, (hereafter cited as *Antiquities*).
3. Ducarel was elected, 4 February 1762, to the Royal Society, not, at this date, exclusively scientific and sharing many members with the Antiquaries. Ducarel was also an honorary founding member of the Society of Antiquaries of Edinburgh (1781), and of the antiquarian societies of Cortonna (1760) and Cassel (1778).
4. I hope to consider Ducarel's official work, mainly that at Lambeth and the books which he produced while there, which follow a different publishing pattern, in my presidential address to the Bibliographical Society.
5. The prints were published in *Vetusta Monumenta* (1747-1893).
6. William Stukeley (1687-1765) FRCP, FSA, FRS, physician and antiquary, dubbed Druid Stukeley from his obsession with Stonehenge and Druidism.
7. Martin Folkes ((1690-1754) FSA, FRS AND DCL: President of the Royal Society (1742) and of the Society of Antiquaries (1750-54); collected gold and silver coins.
8. Smart Letheuillier (1701-60) FRS, FSA, antiquary and collector, early donor to the British Museum.
9. Browne Willis (1682-1760) FSA, DCL, county historian, coin and manuscript collector.
10. Samuel Gale (1682-1754) FRS and FSA, younger brother of a more illustrious antiquary, Roger Gale.
11. LA VI 402. Nichols and Gough bought heavily at the Ducarel sale in April 1786. Much of the material is now in the Bodleian.
12. *Antiquities*, p.ii.

13. George North (1710-72), FSA, numismatist and Vicar of Codicote, letter to Ducarel, 6 July 1752 (John Nichols, *Literary Anecdotes of the Eighteenth Century*, 9 vols, 1712-26. V 456 hereafter cited as LA).

14. In 1713, the year of Andrew's birth, the couple took possession of the Crommelin château of Muids near Les Andelis and Jacques Ducarel took the title of Sieur de Muids.

15. I am indebted to the Squire de Lisle, a descendant of the Doctor's younger nephew, Gerard Augustus Ducarel, for lending me a microfilm of the 1714 Crommelin pedigree, and to Mrs Jean Tsushima for a wealth of information on the family's ramifications as well as help with the intricacies of the French gentry and aristocracy.

16. Manuscript of the *Tour through Normandy* in the hand of an amanuesis with authorial annotations (Gloucestershire Record Office, hereafter cited as GRO, Z1).

17. James to Andrew, July 1764. I am grateful to the Squire de Lisle for shewing me the volume of James's letters (1761-65) which he owns and sending me a transcript (hereafter cited as de Lisle letters).

18. Madame Ducarel's sister had married another wealthy Greenwich Huguenot, M. Pigou, whose money came from the production of gunpowder (information supplied by Mrs Tshushima).

19. It seems that the boys' guardian and trustees established them in a house in Greenwich, with its own staff of servants (Trustee accounts 1732-34, GRO F3).

20. Their tutor was Pierre Issanchon, a strict Calvinist who had been persecuted for his faith and sent to the galleys; he escaped and after many privations reached Switzerland and then came to England and Greenwich where he was employed at a salary of £100 p.a.(E. Haag and E. Haag, *La France Protestante*, 10 vols, 1847-58; Trustee Accounts, GRO F3).

21. The details are not known, but according to Nichols he spent three months receiving treatment in the house of the famous physician Sir Hans Sloane, whose library and antiquities were among the foundation collections of the British Museum.

22. Francis Grose, *The Olio, being a collection of essays... biographical sketches, anecdotes . . . 1791.*

23. He and James matriculated at Trinity College, Oxford in 1731 and 1733 respectively. Andrew moved to St John's, Oxford. James went on to Sidney Sussex College, Cambridge. It was a not uncommon eighteenth-century practice to move from college to college, or even universities.

24. In 1742 their paths diverged; Andrew became DCL; James married a widow, Elizabeth Mary Grafton (Molly) and moved to Ayot St Lawrence, Herts, but they continued to keep in close touch and see a good deal of each other until, in 1761, during the Seven Years' War, James moved to France and began a ten-year battle to regain the family inheritance by establishing residence in France. Finally, in 1771, he acquired the château de Muids from one of his Crommelin cousins, sent for his wife and arranged with Andrew for his English furniture to be sent out to him. The story emerges from the De Lisle letters and those in GRO F5-7.

25. Adrian was protesting against trustee and sibling pressure to send him into a counting house in Amsterdam: 'I see people of some fashion, that are upon a better footing than I can ever expect to be, as bad almost as a foot boy is in England . . .'(GRO F4). He married into a powerful merchant family, the Hamiltons (though the marriage contract is couched in personal and loving terms) and was made a director

of the revived, now respectable South Sea Company at a very young age, which implies influence rather than talent.

26. In letters from friends of their own age, Andrew was 'dear old man', James 'the younker' and Adrian 'cadet'.

27. Letter to Morant 30 June 1757 (BL Add MSS 37, 219, hereafter cited as Morant letters). He first took lodgings in Vauxhall Road and felt an immediate improvement.

28. The John Tradescants, father (d. 1637?) and son (1608-62) travellers, naturalists and gardeners to Charles I, planted a physic garden in the grounds of the Lambeth house which was left to Elias Ashmole. Ducarel also bought a house in Peckham when he married and lived there until 1757. He willed it to his wife.

29. Nichols (LA vi 380), DNB and other authorities call her his maid Susannah but the St Katharine's monument and documents prove otherwise. John Cave-Browne, *Lambeth Palace and its associations*, 1882, calls her Sarah Desborough.

30. John Nichols, *Illustrations of Literature*, 8 vols, 1817-58 (hereafter cited as Ill), iii, 544.

31. From Adrian's younger son, Gerard Augustus Ducarel, 'Gusty', to his uncle James's widow, 22 November 1790, (GRO F4).

32. Thomas Bever (1725-91) scholar and civilian, Doctors Commons, 1758, seems not to have figured in the Doctor's circle, otherwise than as a travelling companion on the 1752 tour. Ducarel recommended him to his Crommelin relations as 'un ami, Docteur en Loix que vous me permetray de vous introduire' (GRO F4).

33. '. . . which is but six posts (about 36 miles) from Rouen, the capital of Upper Normandy; and from thence excellent roads convey the traveller, not only to Paris, which is fifty-five posts . . . but also to other parts of Normandy'. (*Tour through Normandy*, 12; *Anglo-Norman Antiquities Considered* ix).

34. *Tour through Normandy*, 1754, has a charming description of Dover and the journey to Calais, omitted from *Anglo-Norman Antiquities Considered* which eliminates most of the personal diary element of the original.

35. The description in the *Tour*, p.12, differs in some details from that in *Antiquities*, pp.41-2.

36. De Lisle letters August 1764.

37. D. J. A. Matthew is mistaken in saying that Ducarel was the first English writer to see the tapestry ('The English Cultivation of Norman History' *England and Normandy in the Middle Ages*, ed. D. Bates and A. Curry, 1994). Lethieullier saw it first and Ducarel published his description (see p.xx above).

38. GRO F4.

39. *Anglo-Gallic Coins*, preface.

40. GRO F4.

41. De Boze sent two sets, one of which was designated for Dr Mead and duly passed to him. Ducarel extracted the Norman and Aquitain coins (24 in number) and printed them in *Anglo-Gallic Coins*. The album of De Boze's plates, bound in morocco with gilt leaves, was lot 1440 in the sale of Ducarel's library; Gough bought it for £6.10s.

42. North initialled his marginal comments and changes on the draft of the *Tour through Normandy* (GRO Z1), thus providing evidence to disprove Francis Grose's assertion that North ghosted the work. Unscrupulous though Ducarel was in later life in passing off other people's work as his own, there is no evidence that he did so on this occasion. Grose lists all Ducarel's works with their supposed authors (*Olio*, pp.39-49);

but as he asserts the same for all the subjects of his *Olio*, who include Pope and Dr Johnson, this must be taken with a large pinch of salt.

43. Francis Wise (1695-1767) FSA, Radcliffe Librarian at Oxford and author of a dissertation on the White Horse (LA IV 446).

44. Ill IV 447.

45. Ducarel's invariable habit of dating and putting the address of his letters, and of endorsing them with the date of his answer, is invaluable for later scholars.

46. William Derham (1702-57) Professor of Moral Philosophy and President of St John's College, Oxford.

47. GRO Z1; signature illegible.

48. *Anglo-Gallic Coins*, preface.

49. *Anglo-Gallic Coins*, preface.

50. It was on the coins of the Dukes of Brittany and Earls of Richmond, 1066-1404.

51. From a portrait by Antonio Soldi, 1751, in scarlet doctor's robes, engraved by his favourite, Francis Perry. This can be considered equivalent to an author's photograph on the book jacket in our day; but to put the engraving in each of the 47 volumes of manuscript indexes to the archiepiscopal registers was over the top.

52. The work was probably procured for him by his friend, Philip Crespigny (1704-65), Proctor to the Court of Chivalry and of the High Court of Admiralty, member of Doctors Commons, for many years secretary of the South Sea Company. Crespigny was too rich to need to slave away at such work himself.

53. Catalogue of the Harleian Library, vol.2, 1743.

54. Ducarel, following normal eighteenth-century practice, omits the circumflex and is sparing with accents.

55. Ducarel to Milsonneau, 2 July 1752 (GRO F4).

56. I am indebted to Brian North Lee for much information about the Ducarel bookplates. Sotheby's marked file copy, now in the British Library (and microfilmed) gives the immediate whereabouts of most of the books and manuscripts. A huge amount of the papers is now in the Bodleian's Nichols and Gough collections.

57. De Lisle letters.

58. London, 2 vols, 1750. 'I have only quoted the plates mentioned in the Paris edition . . . they are differently numbered in that of London'. (Postscript to the *Tour through Normandy* 39); this, I think, shews that D. J. A. Matthew, *op. cit.*, errs in stating that Ducarel came to Montfaucon in translation. He read French as easily as English, after all.

59. *Anglo-Gallic Coins*, preface.

60. GRO F4.

61. He may have learnt of the work, which he rated high, from Thomas Hollis (1720-74) who knew Abbate Ridolfino Venuti well, mentioned him several times in his diaries and perhaps proposed him for Honorary Fellowship of the Antiquaries.

62. He also found books for the Archbishop, for Philip Crespigny and other friends.

63. Letter to Courtin, 13 May 1756, *op. cit.*, (GRO F4). According to D. J. A. Matthew Ducarel helped to 'give more currency to the term "Anglo-Norman"'.

64. James Bentham (1708-94) prebendary of Ely, author of the great history of Ely Cathedral (1771); letter to Ducarel, 12 March 1757 (CUL Add MSS 1960).

65. It was part of a much larger manuscript, *Monumenta Britannica*, which Aubrey left unpublished at his death in 1695 which circulated widely in antiquary circles.

66. Only two printed copies of *Fashion of Windows* are known — one in the University Library, Cambridge the other in the Royal Institute of British Architects. Gough bought 'a parcel of prints of ancient windows (lot 1367) for 3*s*. 9*d* at the Ducarel sale. Nichols prints the correspondence relating to Ducarel's attempt to publish (*Ill* vi 631-2). The background to the story of the fracas is fully told in the annotation of the RIBA's copy of *Fashion of Windows in Civil and Ecclesiastical Buildings before the Conquest*, in Nicholas Savage *et al.*, *Early Printed Books 1478-1840, Catalogue of the British Architectural Library Early Imprints Collection*, Vol.I., 1994, pp.83-5.

67. Probably Dom Jean Bourget (1724-76) FSA, sub-prior of St Etienne from 1751, who gave or lent his manuscript of the history of the Abbey of Bec to Andrew Ducarel who published an abridged translation (1764). At James's instigation Andrew proposed Bourget for Honorary Fellowship of the Antiquaries (1765).

68. *Antiquities*, p.60.

69. 'Extract of a letter from my Brother James Coltee Ducarel Esq dated Jan 25 1764, containing an account of some Anglo-Norman antiquities considered in ye Abbey of St Stephen at Caen [the most material part thereof is since printed in my *Anglo-Norman Antiquities*]' (Index to Doctor Ducarel's Collections of Original Letters, Papers etc. relative to English & other Antiquities, p.39, (Bodleian Library Gough Misc Antiq. 3-6).

70. *Antiquities*, facing p.49. It was probably fourteenth century, like that surviving at Glastonbury.

71. Letter to Christopher Churchill, 27 March 1764 (Walpole correspondence, ed. W. S. Lewis, 48 vols, 1937-83).

72. 15 January 1763 (De Lisle letters).

73. *Tour through Normandy*, p.36.

74. D. J. A. Matthew, *op. cit.*, p.11.

75. Walpole found him a bore; 'I accepted [Coryate's Poems] to get rid of him t'other day, when he would have talked me to death.' (Walpole correspondence.)

76. Letter to Sir David Dalrymple, 26 October 1768, (Walpole correspondence 15.123). Montfaucon remarked that the costume was clearly later than William's time though the monks believed it to be a portrait of him; Ducarel overlooked Montfaucon's comment when he reproduced the plate.

77. Nichols was printer to the Society of Antiquaries, 1771-98.

78. Dom David Knowles, *The religious orders in England*, vol.II, 1955, includes Ducarel in his bibliography of modern works.

79. See T. W. Bizarro, *Romanesque Architectural Criticism; a Prehistory*, 1991, pp.81-2. *Anglo-Norman Antiquities* was translated by A. L. Lechaude d'Anisy, engineer of Caen and published in a hefty small quarto, with some change of plates, in 1823, and again in 1824. The Society of Antiquaries' copy of the first printing, a gift of the translator, contains a letter of dedication.

The circle of John Gage (1786-1842), Director of the Society of Antiquaries, and the bibliography of medievalism

T. A. BIRRELL

ONE OF THE FEATURES of European Romanticism is the revival of interest in the Middle Ages. This is very easy to point to in German and French literature and history: German and French writers exhibit an emotional, indeed sometimes mystical, affinity with the medieval religious past, and they had a solid mass of eighteenth-century medieval scholarship to back it — principally of course the Benedictines of St Maur and the Bollandists. But in English literature it is very slow in coming: Wordsworth's 'Lines written above Tintern Abbey' (1789) is not about Tintern Abbey at all. Walter Scott's *The Monastery* and *The Abbot* (both of 1820) could scarcely be called sources for a sympathetic understanding of English monasticism: Scott derived his historical information from T. D. Fosbrooke's *British Monachism* (1817).[1] Fosbrooke's approach can be illustrated by his definition of a crypt as 'a place for clandestine drinking, feasting, and things of that kind' and by his conclusion that 'rude ideas, barbarous society, Egyptian superstition, and the Roman Catholic religion, solve all the errors of monasticism'. An informed interest in the totality of medieval culture, religious as well as secular, is none too obvious in the early decades of the nineteenth century: post-Reformation Protestant attitudes died long and hard. It would be reasonable to expect, however, a different attitude among the English Roman Catholics of the period, for whom the Middle Ages were anything but the Dark Ages. In this context the figure of John Gage, a Roman Catholic scholar in a position of some influence, is worth consideration as an 'enlightened' medievalist.

John Gage,[2] born 1786, came from one of the old English Roman Catholic gentry families that went back at least to the fourteenth century and that somehow survived after the Reformation despite active persecution, penal taxation, and a certain amount of in-breeding. In his *History of Hengrave* (1822), Gage very candidly and explicitly points out that the family fortunes were secured by one of his ancestors who was commissioner for the dissolution of the monasteries and who yet remained a Catholic under Henry VIII, Edward VI, and Queen Mary. The family were originally of Firle in Sussex, and a branch established themselves at Hengrave Hall, Bury St Edmunds, in the seventeenth century. John Gage's father was Sir Thomas Gage, sixth baronet, and one of his cousins was Bernard Edward, twelfth Duke of Norfolk, who lived nearby at Fornham Hall.[3] John Gage went to school at Stonyhurst, studied law in the chambers of Charles Butler (1750-1832)[4] and was called to the Bar in 1818, but never practised professionally: he lived most of his life between Hengrave Hall and 10 Old Square, Lincoln's Inn, where he had chambers. Gage moved easily in the circles of the Whig grandees – a welcome visitor at Holland House and Devonshire House, dropping in on Lord Lansdowne at Bowood and on Sir Richard Colt Hoare at Stourhead, and regularly spending Christmas and New Year at shooting parties with Lord Braybrooke at Audley End. He travelled widely and frequently on the Continent: Italy, Holland and Belgium, and France. His travel diaries that have survived are much more than merely those of a tourist: they show a lively intelligence, shrewd observation of people as well as of architecture and paintings and, above all, a gentle self-mockery. Everyone attests to his kindness and sweetness of disposition. He was a confirmed bachelor, always ready to perform services for his relatives and friends: he ran two large estates for members of the family who were minors.[5] An early visitor to the battlefield at Waterloo, he exhumed the body of a young Guards officer who had been killed at Hougomont Farm, the son of a very disagreeable Suffolk neighbour, and took the corpse back with him and buried it in Hengrave Church.[6] He was on very good terms with such difficult characters as Sir Frederick Madden and Sir Thomas Phillipps.[7] In 1838 he inherited the Rokewode estates and changed his name to Gage Rokewode by Private Act of Parliament. He died of a stroke while out on a shooting party, at the early age of 56 years.

So much for his character and social setting, both of which are important in what follows. Over and above that, he was a remarkable scholar – he was not a dilettante in the pejorative sense of the word 'antiquarian'. In her *History of the Society of Antiquaries*, Joan Evans says of Gage that he was intelligent, a term that she uses very sparingly. Gage was never merely content to describe an object, or merely to buttress his description with a mass of learned references – he always wanted to compare it or relate it to something else, and very often to quite different kinds of objects. His publications are on very disparate topics, yet he seems to have a kind of hidden agenda, which might be described as the cultural anthropology of the Middle Ages.

Gage was elected Fellow of the Society of Antiquaries in 1818 and became Director of the Society in 1829 (coincidentally the year of the Catholic Emancipation Act). He remained Director for thirteen years until his unexpectedly early death. The duties of Director were defined in 1737 as:

the superintendence and custody of the Society's drawings, engravings and books, the management and sale of its publications of prints and books, and the delivery to each member of those due to him. The Director was to approve of drawings and inscriptions before they were engraved, to have the custody of the copper-plates, and to deliver the printing accounts quarterly to the Treasurer. Further he was to be the custodian of the Society's collections.[8]

By the time of Gage's Directorship there was added the editorship of the Society's journal, *Archaeologia*, founded in 1769, and of the occasional series *Vetusta Monumenta*. Anyone who has ever had the experience of being the editor of a learned journal knows that it is the best way of making enemies for life — and anyone who knows anything about the Society of Antiquaries in the early nineteenth century knows that there were plenty of enemies waiting to be made. But Gage sailed through unruffled: there is not a hint of trouble during his long tenure of office.

The minutes of the Society show that a great deal of his time was certainly involved in matters concerning the engraving of plates, indeed the Society must have been a substantial patron of engravers and artists. But before we deal with Gage's editorship of *Archaeologia*, and his own publications, we should consider Gage's role in another publication project of the Society: the publication of Anglo-Saxon poetic texts.[9]

It is a commonplace generalization that after the great days of Anglo-Saxon scholarship from the sixteenth to the early eighteenth century, from Archbishop Parker and Lawrence Nowell to Hickes and Wanley, the English did nothing about their Anglo-Saxon literature, and it was left to the Icelanders, the Danes and the Germans. To be sure, the Icelandic scholar Grimur Thorkelin (1752-1829) had transcribed *Beowulf* in 1786 and translated it into Latin in 1815, and N. F. S. Grundtvig (1783-1872) had translated *Beowulf* into Danish in 1820 and had visited Exeter Cathedral to transcribe the *Exeter Book* and claimed, quite falsely, to be the first person to have consulted it since the Middle Ages. In 1830 Grundtvig had the temerity to issue a prospectus: *Bibliotheca Anglo-Saxonica. Prospectus and proposals of a subscription for the most valuable Anglo-Saxon manuscripts illustrative of the early poetry and literature of our* [sic] *language, most of which have never been printed.* The Antiquaries determined that this had got to be stopped: they wanted texts with translations, and Grundtvig's command of modern English was totally inadequate. In 1831 they issued a rival prospectus—from the same publisher, Black, Young and Young—and Grundtvig went back to Denmark to join Kierkegaard as an early existentialist theologian. The Antiquaries' prospectus proposed, for a start, the publication of *Caedmon*, the *Exeter Book* and *Layamon's Brut*: text with translation *en face*. Lord Aberdeen and Hudson Gurney, President and Vice-President, put up some of the money, Sir Henry Ellis, the Secretary, supported it and, as we shall see, it fitted in perfectly with the interests of John Gage, the Director.

One of Gage's great friends was the Catholic historian John Lingard (1771-1851),[10] whose first published work was *The Antiquities of the Anglo-Saxon Church* (Newcastle 1806, 1810 and London 1845).[11] Lingard's considerable, and very unbuttoned, correspondence with Gage reveals *inter alia* that Gage handled Lingard's financial affairs when his publisher went bankrupt. Lingard's approach to medieval church history is exemplified in the conclusion of his preface to the 1845 edition: 'With the truth or falsehood of doctrine I have no concern: my object is to discover and establish facts.' His style, and weapon, is Gibbonian irony.[12]

The Antiquaries' plan to publish Anglo-Saxon poetic records, text and translation *en face*, was exactly what Gage wanted, to provide evidence of a vernacular and sophisticated Anglo-Saxon religious literary culture to back up Lingard's history of the Anglo-Saxon Church. The editor of *Caedmon* and the *Exeter Book* was Benjamin Thorpe (1782-1870), who had studied Anglo-Saxon at Copenhagen with Rasmus Raske. Thorpe wanted to publish Anglo-Saxon religious prose texts as well—an undertaking outside the Antiquaries' remit—so he decided to form an Aelfric Society for the purpose of publishing Aelfric's *Homilies* for a start. (It was of course the great age for the founding of publishing societies.) Thorpe printed a prospectus and sent it to Gage for financial support: Gage approved and passed it on to Lingard. Now Aelfric's *Homilies* had interested Archbishop Parker in the sixteenth century because Aelfric had apparently proposed a view of the Real Presence in the Eucharist which corresponded with that of the early Protestant reformers. Lingard sent his subscription without any hesitation: his primary concern was to have the texts in print.[13]

It is now time to consider a few of Gage's own publications. *Archaeologia* 24 (1832) contained an article by Gage of 136 pages and 32 plates on *The Benedictional of St. Aethelwold*, that masterpiece of eleventh-century Anglo-Saxon art (he subsequently reprinted it as a separate large-paper volume: the trick was to get the Antiquaries to pay for the plates).[14] The *Benedictional* belonged at that time to William Cavendish, sixth Duke of Devonshire: in 1720 Humfrey Wanley had tried to buy it for the Harleian Library but had been rebuffed by the then Duke.[15] Gage was able to edit it because of his social contacts with Devonshire House: it would seem that the Duke simply sent the manuscript to Gage's chambers in Lincoln's Inn, and let Gage send the manuscript on to the engraver. Gage's introduction is purely factual – he begins by explaining what a Benedictional was, and introducing the reader to the continental literature on the subject. Most important of all, he establishes the concept of a Winchester school of illumination and compares the volume with a similar Winchester Pontifical in the Public Library at Rouen. For an aesthetic valuation of the manuscript he relies on extensive quotation from the opinions of W. Y. Ottley, a dealer, collector and connoisseur.[16] The publication made a great impression on Lingard:

I admire much the research and judgement which you display in your preliminary dissertation, but still more (without disparagement to you) that extraordinary change in the public mind which has permitted the Antiquarian Society to publish under its auspices so papistical a treatise.[17]

But perhaps Lingard missed the point. It was precisely because Gage's introduction was so calm and factual, without any 'enthusiasm' (in the eighteenth-century sense), and without any verbiage, that the Antiquaries could accept and publish it. The key to the significance of John Gage lies not only in what he did, but in the way that he did it.

Gage was also concerned with architecture, and protested against the proposed destruction of the screen at York Minster, and the demolition of the Lady Chapel at St Saviour's Southwark.[18] Of course, it was rather embarrassing for a Roman Catholic to protest at alterations in what were Protestant places of worship, but Gage's protests were always extremely polite, factual and informative, unlike the strident polemics of a fellow Roman Catholic, Bishop John Milner (1752-1826), in his protests at the alterations in Winchester and Salisbury cathedrals.[19] Kenneth Clark has rightly called Milner 'a popish wolf in the guise of an antiquarian sheep'[20] – Milner did certainly *not* belong to the circle of John Gage. In his travel diaries Gage shows that his architectural taste was remarkably eclectic. He had no faith in the perfection of one particular, absolute style – that is, Gothic. What he sought were combinations of style and period that were aesthetically harmonious – something which Pevsner has pointed to as being characteristic of the Englishness of English art.[21]

Gage was also interested in the archaeology of the Anglo-Saxon church. In *Archaeologia* 26 (1836) he published an article on 'Sepulchral stones found at Hartlepool in 1833', which gives evidence for a monastic graveyard in the North East in the age of Bede. The stones had runic inscriptions, and the subsequent publication of J. M. Kemble's pioneering 50-page article on Anglo-Saxon runes in *Archaeologia* 28 (1840) was clearly part of Gage's editorial policy: Kemble's is the first systematic printed treatment of runes in any language.

Another instance of Gage's editorial policy was his article in *Archaeologia* 28 (1839) on what is now known as the Bedford Psalter[22] (as distinct from the Bedford Hours). It was owned by another of the old Catholic gentry families, the Welds of Lulworth Castle: Gage persuaded Joseph Weld to exhibit it at the Antiquaries. The Weld family had given the Stonyhurst estate to the Jesuits in 1794 to found the school which Gage had attended – indeed, he must have been one of the first pupils. This is a very good example of the old school tie influencing the publication of rare medieval artefacts in private hands. It is therefore surprising to read in Edward Miller's history of the British Museum that the existence of the Bedford Psalter 'was not suspected by students until it was brought into the Museum [in 1928] for an opinion, but it now ranks as one of its greatest treasures'.[23] Perhaps Miller's ignorance is due to the fact that Gage, in his innate modesty, published his brief account of the Bedford Psalter in the appendix to *Archaeologia*, so that it does not appear in the table of contents at the front.

Joseph Weld also owned the famous Luttrell Psalter[24] which Gage published on the grand scale in another series of the Antiquaries, *Vetusta Monumenta* (1842) – Gage had revived the series and after his directorship it was discontinued for 60 years. The Luttrell Psalter is a perfect example of the combination of the secular with the religious in medieval culture: it was a Gallican psalter and all things Gallican were much more acceptable to the Anglican clergy than all things Roman. In his description Gage concentrates primarily on the provenance of the manuscript.

Another publication of Gage in *Vetusta Monumenta* was *The Painted Chamber in the Palace of Westminster* (1842) with fourteen plates. Again, with characteristic modesty, Gage describes his article as a reconsideration of the drawings of Charles Stothard (1786-1821), commissioned by the Antiquaries and presented to the Society in a paper in 1820. In fact, Gage's article completely supersedes Stothard, and is a very distinguished piece of art history. Gage gives an aesthetic analysis of the drawings themselves, linking them stylistically with analogies to English miniature paintings and other English medieval illuminations, and he knows enough about Italian art to dismiss Stothard's suggestions of Italian influence. Gage sent specimens of the paint to Michael Faraday for analysis and dating, and conducted two archaeological investigations of the site. But most important of all, he combines all this with the archival sources, which Stothard never did. By using the evidence of the Close Rolls and the Liberate Rolls of Henry III, and expense accounts of 1306 from Edward II (a manuscript borrowed from Sir Thomas Phillipps), Gage shows that the paintings derive from two periods and, furthermore, that the archival materials enable us to give the medieval artists an identity. The most recent study of the Painted Chamber is by Dr Paul Binski, in an Occasional Paper of the Society of Antiquaries (new series 9 of 1986), based on a Cambridge thesis. Dr Binski is most generous in his assessment of Gage's work:

Striking comparative material is chosen from contemporary English manuscripts, such as the Guthlac Roll, the lives of the Offas, and the Queen Mary Psalter, works which a generation earlier would have invited scorn, but which are here accurately reproduced. . . . In effect, Gage had a view recognizable by modern art historians of the *milieu* of medieval paintings at Westminster . . . Gage's account of the Painted Chamber attests to the remarkable progress in the study of medieval English art in the period 1820-1840.[25]

The only point that might be added is that the availability of archival sources would have been impossible without Gage's friendly relationship with Sir Thomas Phillipps, and also with Henry Petrie (1768-1842), Keeper of the Records in the Tower.

Gage's residence at Hengrave Hall involved him in an interest in the history of the great monastery at Bury St Edmunds. In 1838 he published his first and only volume of the *History of Suffolk: Thingoe*

Hundred. As far as the medieval history of Suffolk was concerned, this shows how the Abbey of St Edmund completely dominated the county: only the Franciscans dared to try to establish themselves in the area, and they got pretty short shrift. Apart from cartularies and other estate papers, the Abbey of St Edmund produced one great human document, the *Chronicle* of Jocelin of Brakelond (BL Harley MS 1005). Gage's publication of this involved one of his closest friends, a man nearly 20 years his junior, Thomas Stapleton (1805-49) of Carlton Towers, Yorkshire: Carlton Towers must be one of the few estates that had passed down by direct inheritance through the same family since the Norman Conquest.[26] Like Gage, Stapleton was from a very old Roman Catholic family, like Gage he was a serious medieval scholar, like Gage he was a friend of Sir Thomas Phillipps, and like Gage he died young. Stapleton was an expert in the arcane field of the Norman Exchequer Rolls, published by the Society of Antiquaries in two volumes, *Magni Rotuli Scaccarii Normanniae sub Regibus Angliae* (1841-4). There are over 500 pages of introduction, which are still referred to today as the major authority on the subject. Most of Stapleton's work was published after Gage's death, and includes studies of medieval religious houses. He became Vice-President of the Society of Antiquaries in 1846.[27]

Now Stapleton was one of the founder members of the Camden Society—Lord Braybrooke was another. In the Camden Society committee's prospectus of 1838, they list the first fifteen volumes. Volume one was already published and volumes two to four were in the press: volume four was a substantial collection of family letters, the *Plumpton Correspondence*, edited by Stapleton himself.[28] Among the volumes advertised as 'in progress' was volume thirteen (actually published in 1840) which, unlike any other publication of the Camden Society, has the title entirely in Latin: *Chronica Jocelini de Brakelond, de rebus Gestis Samsonis abbati monasterii Sancti Edmundi. Nunc primum typis mandata curante Johanne Gage Rokewode.* It is obvious that Stapleton had leant very heavily on his friend John Gage to produce a volume in a hurry to help to get the infant Camden Society off the ground. Gage had had a transcript of the manuscript by him for some time, as part of his materials for the continuation of his history of the county of Suffolk: he added a very brief introduction and a minimum of annotation, but he had had no time for a translation. Gage knew that it was a wonderful human document, as well as a major contribution to twelfth-century monastic history, but he did not waste time enthusing about it. His preface concludes:

The style of the work is easy, mixed, but not offensively, with the language of writers sacred and profane, according to the custom of the monastic historians of the age. The story is told throughout with a pleasing naïveté, and sometimes humour: the characters are drawn with spirit, and the whole seems written with truth.

Gage's objective scholarly edition was read by the very unobjective and unscholarly historian Thomas Carlyle (1795-1881), who published *Past and Present* in 1843. This was a kind of diptych in which 'the past' was represented by the great single-minded Abbot Samson of St Edmund's Abbey, contrasted with 'the present', the world of the venal little pettifoggers of the day – Carlyle got the trick from A. W. Pugin's *Contrasts* (1836) which set highly idealized pictures of medieval buildings and towns over against highly lurid pictures of modern buildings and factory towns. Carlyle's popularization, or rather vulgarization, of Jocelin's *Chronicle* created the market for a translation. This was produced in the following year (1844) by Thomas Edlyne Tomlins (1804-72) in a kind of early paperback series, Whittakers Popular Library, badly printed in double columns.[29] Tomlins's preface, ironically enough, was written in the spirit of T. D. Fosbrooke. The great Felix Liebermann edited extracts from Gage's edition in the *Monumenta Germaniae Scriptorum* (vol.27), with a charming preface praising Gage's scholarship and accuracy – Liebermann was an inveterate Anglophile. Thomas Arnold, Matthew Arnold's younger brother and professor at the Catholic University of Dublin, re-edited the text for the Rolls Series (1890); there was a new translation in the delightful Kings Classics series (1903) published by the De La More press; and in 1949 a definitive edition by H. E. Butler with Latin text and translation *en face*. In his modest and quiet way, to please a friend, Gage had put into circulation a document of wide general modern appeal, the most outstanding biography of the English Middle Ages.

During the latter years of Gage's life, he developed a friendship with Dr Daniel Rock (1799-1871). Like Gage, Rock hobnobbed with the Whig grandees, corresponded with Sir Thomas Phillipps, and lived for a time at Alton Towers as private chaplain to John Talbot, sixteenth Earl of Shrewsbury, who was to be the great patron of A. W. Pugin. Rock was a liturgiologist and an ecclesiologist. In his conversation and in his correspondence he was somewhat different from Gage, Lingard,

Stapleton or Weld; his approach was, one might say, pastoral – he was quite open about his emotional attachment to the Middle Ages. But when he sat at his desk, he was the objective scholar. In 1833 he published *Hierurgia*,[30] which was the first scholarly treatise on the Mass to be published in England since the Reformation. As the very possession of Mass books in England, let alone their publication, had been prohibited by law, there had been a complete scholarly blank for over two centuries. Rock's book brought the fruits of continental liturgical scholarship to the attention of English readers. It is worth remembering that the Cambridge Camden Society (later the Ecclesiological Society), the first Anglican circle of influence for the scholarly study of ritual, was not founded till 1839. Rock's book was republished in 1851 and again in 1893, the latter edition was by W. H. J. Weale. Weale's edition became part of an ecumenical series, the Catholic Standard Library, published by John Hodges of Henrietta Street (later of Agar Street, Charing Cross), which included High Anglican as well as Roman Catholic books. Indeed, one of Rock's later books, *The Church of Our Fathers* (1849), a treatise on the Sarum Rite, was announced by Hodges as being re-edited by 'the Benedictines of Downside', but was in fact re-edited in 1903 by G. W. Hart and W. H. Frere, two Anglican priests of the Community of the Resurrection at Mirfield.[31] With the transitional figure of Daniel Rock one realizes that the ethos of John Gage belonged very firmly to the first half of the nineteenth century.

This brief survey of a selection of his publications should be enough to indicate a line, a policy, a hidden agenda, in the career of one man, John Gage, whose combined social and scholarly status was most unusual. This is not necessarily to imply that there were not other medievalists of the period with comparable qualifications and with comparable aims. What is being suggested is that Gage's cultural-anthropological approach to the religious life of the Middle Ages is something we can recognize and appreciate today.

References

1. Other editions 1802 and 1843.
2. The bulk of Gage's voluminous correspondence and other papers are in the Hengrave Hall Deposit, Cambridge University Library. Some other personal items are among the Hengrave Estate papers at Suffolk Record Office, Bury St Edmunds. His travel diary for Wiltshire is in the Wiltshire R.O., Trowbridge. I am most grateful to Peter Meadows and Giles Mandelbrote for their help.

3. John Martin Robinson, *The Dukes of Norfolk* (Oxford, 1982), p.189.

4. The late Nigel Abercrombie was engaged on a biography of Charles Butler. His article 'The early life of Charles Butler', *Recusant History*, 14 (1978), 281-92, gives some idea of Butler's social background.

5. Alan Merryman, 'Portrait on the Stairs', *Hengrave News*, Spring 1990, 7-10. I am most grateful to Sister Julian of the Hengrave Hall Centre for sending me this article.

6. See ' "A Sentimental Journey" through Holland and Flanders by John Gage' in Susan Roach (ed.), *Across the Narrow Seas: Studies in the History and Bibliography of Britain and the Low Countries Presented to Anna E. C. Simoni* (London, 1991).

7. Besides being a bigot and a bully, Phillipps was a tuft-hunter. In an age acutely conscious of social status, he knew full well that Sir Thomas Phillipps, first Baronet and bastard son of a Manchester cotton-manufacturer, was socially inferior to John Gage, Esquire. The Phillipps correspondence is in the Bodleian.

8. Joan Evans, *History of the Society of Antiquaries* (Oxford, 1956), p.86.

9. For a fuller account see 'The Society of Antiquaries and the taste for Old English 1705-1840', *Neophilologus*, 50 (1966), 107-18.

10. M. Haile and E. Bonney, *Life and Letters of John Lingard* (London, [1911]), do not use the Gage correspondence.

11. It is characteristic of the 'medievalism' of the period that the titlepage of the first edition of Lingard's book boasts a Bewick wood-engraving depicting ivy-covered ruins and a warrior on horseback brandishing a spear.

12. The following footnote, on the early hermits of the Egyptian desert, is characteristic: 'As early as the commencement of the second century, we discover members of both sexes who had devoted themselves to a life of perpetual celibacy. Yet the sagacity of Mosheim has discovered that this practice owes its origin not to the doctrine of the Gospel, but to the influence of the climate of Egypt. If this be true, we must admire the heroism of the present inhabitants, who in their harems have subdued the influence of the climate, and introduced the difficult practice of polygamy, in lieu of the easy virtue of chastity'.

13. CUL MS Hengrave Hall Deposit 21 (13), 23 July 1841, (the volumes are not foliated).

14. Subsequently republished by G. F. Warner and H. A. Wilson (eds), London, 1910 and F. Wormald (ed.), London, 1959.

15. C. E. and R. C. Wright (eds), *The Diary of Humfrey Wanley* (London, 1966), pp.19, 106-7; cf. *British Museum Quarterly*, 27 (1963), 3-5.

16. A. N. L. Munby, *Connoisseurs and Mediaeval Miniatures* (Oxford, 1972), pp.62-8, 140.

17. Quoted in Evans (*op. cit.* note 8), p.235, from CUL MS Hengrave Hall, Deposit 21 (4).

18. *Remarks on the Alterations proposed in York Minster* (London, 1831).

19. John Milner, *History of the Antiquities of Winchester* (Winchester, 1798-1801); *Short View of the History . . . of Winchester* (Winchester, 1799, 1802, 1812); *Dissertation on the Modern Style of altering Ancient Cathedrals, as exemplified in the Cathedral of Salisbury* (London, 1798; Winchester, 1811). Milner was associated with the even more polemical John Carter, for whom see J. Mordaunt Crook, *John Carter and the Mind of the Gothic Revival* (London, 1995), esp. pp.11, 27.

20. *The Gothic Revival* (revised ed. London, 1950), pp.140-1.

21. Gage's unpublished notes on Winchester Cathedral are characteristic: 'The imagination is perhaps more alive here than in any other cathedral in England. The *coup d'oeil* embracing Beaufort's, Waynflete's and Fox's monuments with the different chapels, lights, painted glass and ornament and loft roofs, is perhaps not to be equalled anywhere else' (Wiltshire R.O., MS 2606/1, leaves unfoliated).

22. Now BL MS Add. 42131.

23. Edward Miller, *That Noble Cabinet: a History of the British Museum* (London, 1973), p.342.

24. Now BL MS Add. 42130: later published by Eric George Millar (London, 1932) and Janet Backhouse (London, 1989).

25. P. Binski, *The Painted Chamber at Westminster* (London, 1986), pp.23, 30-1.

26. John Martin Robinson, *Carlton Towers* (London, 1991).

27. The index to E. B. Graves, *Bibliography of English History to 1485* (Oxford, 1975), gives a good impression of the range of Stapleton's publications.

28. It covered the history of a family before, during and after the Reformation, analogous to Sir John Fenn's edition of the Paston letters (1767-1823) though not so interesting. The Plumpton letters were in the possession of yet another old Catholic family, the Towneleys.

29. Whittaker's stocklist included Michelet's *History of France*; Ranke's *History of the Popes*; Stow's *Survey of London* (ed. W. J. Thoms); Thiers's *History of the French Revolution*; and Thierry's *History of the Conquest of England by the Normans*. The paperback volumes could also be had 'handsomely bound in cloth and letters at 1s. extra'.

30. Although 'hierurgia' is more strictly accurate than 'liturgia', the word never caught on.

31. I have not yet been able to find out much about the firm of John Hodges. The Catholic Standard Library (at 12 shillings per volume) was a late nineteenth-century series including Anglican editions of Cornelius à Lapide, Maldonatus S.J., Bernardine à Picino, and St Bernard of Clairvaux, besides S. R. Maitland's *The Dark Ages* (first ed. 1844), a lively and brilliant rehabilitation of medieval religious culture, by the Librarian at Lambeth Palace. As well as Rock's major works, other Roman Catholic books included Cardinal Gasquet's *Henry VIII and the English Monasteries*; Gasquet and Edmund Bishop's *Edward VI and the Book of Common Prayer*; and Pastor's *History of the Popes vols I-IV* (the series was later taken over by Kegan Paul – an unlikely publisher for so papistical a work – and completed in 40 volumes in 1953).

Bibliotheca Heberiana

Arnold Hunt

IS THE COLLECTOR naturally at home in circles of learning, or is collecting, as is often suggested, an essentially private pursuit? The life of Richard Heber highlights the distinction in a particularly acute form. After Heber's death his friends were naturally anxious to defend his reputation, and insisted that, despite appearances, his vast library of 150,000 volumes had served a useful social purpose. 'There are doubtless many persons of the present generation,' sniffed the *Gentleman's Magazine* in April 1836, 'a generation so confident in its march of intellect, who think it absurd and useless for any one to devote his attention to the collecting ancient writings and antiquities, for perusal and study.' But without 'the careful guardians of ancient books, in each succeeding century', the literature of the past would not have come down to us:

The works of Peele, Greene, Marlow, and others of our early dramatic poets, have been collected together, and published within the last few years. Had it not been for the curious libraries formed by Mr Heber, and other admirers of Old English literature, these publications could not have been produced; for, in many instances, portions of them have been printed from the original or only editions, of which perhaps only one copy existed.[1]

But posterity took a very different view of Heber. Chambers's *Book of Days* presented Heber to the Victorian reader as a slave to biblio-mania, a man who collected books 'merely for the pleasure of collecting' and made no effort to put them at the service of others.

When he died, curiosity was naturally excited to know what provision he had made in reference to his immense store of books; but when his will was discovered, after a long and almost hopeless search among bills, notes, memoranda, and letters, it was found, to the astonishment of every one on reading it, that the library was *not even mentioned!* It seemed as if Heber cared nothing what should become of the books, or who should possess them after his decease; and as he was never married, or influenced greatly by domestic ties, his

Heber in defeat. Pencil drawing by J. Harris, *c.*1831-33. [NPG 4886.]
Reproduced by permission of the National Portrait Gallery, London.

library was considered by the executors of his will as merely so much 'property', to be converted into cash by the aid of the auctioneer.

'We can hardly come to any other conclusion,' added Chambers severely, 'than that Mr Heber's life was nearly a useless one – performing unnecessary work, which was undone soon after his death.'[2]

It is not easy to choose between these two alternatives. Even Heber's friends were sometimes baffled by the contradictions in his character: 'Mr Heber is a "Man of Mystery"', wrote T. F. Dibdin, 'and there is no making "head or tail" of him'. One obituary of Heber observed that 'so many different stories' were told about him 'that it is scarcely possible to ascertain accurately what is true, and what is false'. The task is no easier today. Many, though not all, of Heber's papers have been preserved and are now in the Bodleian, but Heber was not a man who habitually committed his thoughts to paper: 'I am a bad *gossip* with a pen to my hand,' he told a friend, 'and generally confine myself therefore to matters of business.'[3] Most of his surviving letters are brief and impersonal, and one is forced to rely heavily on other people's testimony – their letters to, letters about and recollections of him, with Dibdin's letters to Lord Spencer providing the ground bass – to supplement the meagre stock of Heber's own words. I will concentrate on Heber's character as much as on his library, because his character is so fascinating and so enigmatic, and it is impossible to make sense of the one without knowing something about the other.

Richard Heber was born in 1774, the eldest son of a well-off, well-connected Shropshire gentry family, high Tory and solidly Church of England. His father, Reginald Heber, was a prosperous country clergyman, a former fellow of Brasenose College, Oxford, and Rector of Malpas in Cheshire and Hodnet in Shropshire, both family livings, which he held in plurality. His mother, Mary Heber (*née* Baylie), died when he was three months old, which may partly account for his rather introverted character. Richard's formative years are vividly portrayed in A. N. L. Munby's 'Father and Son', subtitled 'The Rev. Reginald Heber's vain attempt to stem the rising tide of his son Richard's bibliomania'.[4] Reginald, as Munby shows, held firm and decided views on book collecting: 'A small collection of well chosen books are sufficient for the entertainment and instruction of every man, and all else are useless lumber.' His pride in his son's literary pursuits quickly gave way to alarm, and in 1789 there was a serious row when he found that Richard had been buying books without his permission. 'Your

Booksellers' Bills within these last two years amount to the sum of seventy pounds', he informed his son. 'I am determin'd to put a stop to this extravagance . . . and you will displease me exceedingly if you persist in it.'

Outwardly, at least, the relationship between Richard and his father was certainly affectionate, and one contemporary even recalled seeing Reginald, 'a tall and handsome clergyman, in middle life', accompanying his son to the auction rooms.[5] However, one cannot help being struck by the contrast between the formality of Richard's letters to his father and the much lighter tone of the correspondence with his aunt Elizabeth in London, who seems to have been almost a surrogate mother to him. Richard's letters to his father describe his activities in some detail but very rarely mention his book collecting, and the repeated appeals for cash to settle his debts somehow contrive to ignore his father's requests for a full statement of his expenditure. His letters to his aunt, on the other hand, entrust her with small errands such as sending him catalogues or reporting the results of sales, and are generally much more informative about his collecting activities. For her part, Elizabeth Heber clearly doted on her nephew. When the influenza came to London she fretted about Richard's health: 'it is next to impossible any Body can Escape who comes to Town at this time; and attends such *Places as Book Sales*. Let your Purchases be made by substitutes and *keep your Self* out of harms Way.' She allowed Richard to store his new acquisitions in her house, and seems to have coped admirably with the minor domestic inconveniences that ensued, as when crates of books arrived unexpectedly from Strasburg, or importunate bibliophiles turned up at her door demanding admittance. 'Mr Park was here yesterday morning', she reported to her nephew in 1802, 'to search for Willoughbys Avisa a small quarto Volume which He sais He is sure is in your Possession, that you Purchased it at Steevens's Sale & that He knows not to whom to applie for it as it cannot be found amongst your Books in this House . . . Park had been with Bindly & Malone who neither of them have it. He means to go to the Museum to obtain a sight of it if there, not knowing how to go on without it.'[6]

Several aspects of Richard's personality emerge from the family correspondence. The first is his personal charm. 'His cheerfulness and the charms of his conversation,' wrote one of his obituarists, 'supplied with a fund of amusing anecdote, rendered him a most acceptable and delightful companion.' He lacked his half-brother Reginald's gift for storytelling, and his humour is often of a slightly donnish variety, but the desire to please, the desire to entertain, are very much apparent in his early letters. Many of these are included in a volume of family correspondence entitled *The Heber Letters*, published in 1950, which contains little bibliographical information but is still well worth getting hold of, not least for the charming frontispiece of the future book-collector at the age of eight, complete with shoulder-length hair and cricket bat.[7] (The portrait, by John Singleton Copley, is now in the Yale Centre for British Art.) In later life he was a member of several London clubs, including the exclusive dining society known simply as 'the Club' of which Dr Johnson had been a member, the Athenaeum, of which he was one of the founders, and of course the Roxburghe Club,[8] but not, significantly, the Society of Antiquaries.

Already, though, there are disconcerting hints of another side to his character. He was often secretive, particularly about his book collecting: it is clear that he was attending auctions throughout the 1790s and buying books on an increasingly lavish scale, yet in 1796 he assures his father that he has contracted no new debts and has not lapsed into 'ancient extravagances'. He could be reticent, often to his own disadvantage and perhaps to the point of deceit, as in 1821 when he stood for Parliament and, to the amazement of many of his friends, declared himself opposed to Catholic emancipation. 'The consistency, or the integrity of this declaration, is matter with himself', remarked Dibdin darkly. 'But, there is a strong sensation abroad, that he once thought *otherwise* . . . I fear he has been *trimming.*' There are also suggestions of an underlying loneliness and insecurity, not just in his urge to surround himself with books but in his equally compulsive urge to travel. He was constantly on the move between London, Oxford and Shropshire, never staying in one place for long. 'On hearing of a curious book,' wrote one obituarist, 'he has been known to put himself into the mail coach, and travel three, four, or five hundred miles to obtain it, fearful to entrust his commission to a letter.'[9]

Reginald Heber the elder died in 1804, and it was only then that Richard began to collect books on a serious scale. Until 1804 he was living on a quarterly allowance of £100; after 1804 he was in sole possession of the Yorkshire, Shropshire and Norfolk estates, with an annual income approaching the proverbial 'ten thousand a year'. As his friend Walter Scott remarked prophetically in 1806: 'His father being now dead and he in possession of a large property, his diligence indefatigable and his taste undoubted he will be soon in possession of the noblest library in England.'[10] Heber's effective collecting career lasted for only 30 years (he was 60 when he died) but for a collector of ample means it was a period of exceptional opportunity. Books were in plentiful supply, thanks in part to the eighteenth-century collectors like Isaac Reed and George Steevens whose libraries were fresh on the market, in part to the dispersal of monastic libraries on the Continent, and in part to the high prices that attracted books into the London bookshops and salerooms.

Apart from a healthy bank balance, Heber's principal asset in collecting books was his own phenomenal memory. In 1816 he wrote a remarkable letter to his friend Edward Copleston telling him where to find a set of 'the treatises of Funccius on the several ages of the Latin Language':

If you will take the trouble to go to my lodgings, (Mrs Adams will I doubt not, give you admittance – provided her daughters be in another part of the house) you will find them bound in 5 volumes, small quarto, rather thick, in vellum covers, standing to the best of my recollection, on a *lower, right-hand* shelf, of the *white-painted* bookcase, *opposite the windows*, in the *room* at the head of the back staircase.[11]

What makes this feat of memory even more remarkable is that Heber kept his books in several different locations, subject to constant rearrangement. Most of his books, of course, were bought in London. They were stored in the house in Westminster which had belonged to his aunt Elizabeth and which, after her death in 1812, became what one writer called 'Mr Heber's warehouse, or usual depository for books as soon as purchased; here he used to arrange them, selecting those which he considered fit either for the house at Pimlico or for his country residence.'[12] His collection of English poetry, and his bibliographical reference library, were kept in his main London residence at Pimlico. Other books went to Hodnet Hall, the most valuable going by the mail coach as part of Heber's hand luggage, the rest in boxes by the Shrewsbury carrier. The lodgings that he mentions in his letter to Copleston were, however, in Oxford, and seem, like the house in Westminster, to have been a clearing-house for books on their way to Pimlico or Hodnet. 'Paid for carriage of the above from Oxford to Shrewsbury', reads a note on one of Heber's booklists, '£7.7.0 which I suspect to be a gross imposition. Gave the man at Oxford who packed them 10.6 besides paying him for the paper bought to pack them.'[13] It is clear from his notes that he supervised every detail, from 'packed up under my inspection' at one end of the journey to 'arranged in the Library by myself' at the other. Heber took great care of his books: there is a delightful anecdote of his reserving all the inside seats on the mail coach for his books, 'not losing sight of them until they arrived at their destination, and watching them with the greatest anxiety during the whole of the journey' (history does not relate the feelings of the passengers on the outside of the coach).[14] When books were sent to him from abroad, he went personally to the custom-house to collect them, 'as I chuse to see the goods weighed and delivered myself'.[15] When he sent books to be bound, his instructions stipulated the precise wording and spacing of the lettering on the spine, and when they returned from the binders he took care to scrutinize the bill.[16]

The editions of the Greek and Latin classics formed the backbone of Heber's library. These were the first books he collected, sup-plemented by further collections of modern Latin poetry (inaugurated at the Fazakerley sale in 1801[17]) and classical history and philology. In 1826, when Heber was on the Continent, he ordered from London a small group of modern books that may have been intended as a travelling library: they included Dibdin's *Bibliographical Tour* of France and Germany, his friend Martin Routh's collection of patristic texts *Reliquiae Sacrae*, and nine volumes of classical Greek plays. This, it seems, was Heber's preferred reading; his desert island collection, one might say. One tends to think of Heber as, above all, a collector of English literature, but the Greek and Latin classics came first and it is fair to say that they provided him with a standard against which to judge all other literature. The highest compliment he could pay Scott's poem *Marmion* was to compare the description of the Scottish army in Canto IV to the 'catalogues of ships and armies' in the classical epics.[18] Heber was one of the founders of the *Quarterly Review*, and there seems little doubt that he would have supported the *Quarterly*'s attack on Keats's Cockney rhymes. His taste in poetry was decidedly conservative, Augustan (in both the classical and the eighteenth-century sense) in its insistence upon strict accuracy. He chided Scott for treating the word 'real' as one syllable rather than two, and subjected his half-brother Reginald's poem *Europe*, which he read in draft, to a withering critique on the grounds of banality and mixed metaphor:

The lines you sent, were certainly hurried off, under the continued disadvantage of a lovesick fit, & the horrors of invading Methodism. The 2 introductory lines which promise remarkably well, are fitted to others which seem not to have been intended to unite with them. To tell Spain, whom you justly term virtuous brave & majestic that she is first in every fight, & that she is found bending with patient beauty over the wound of the soldier, is investing her with attributes, is giving her what in my opinion seems more properly to be the business of a personified being like Spanish Patriotism, or Spanish Liberty, or Spain's good genius. You make Spain an abject part of herself. And the concluding hope that the rational liberty of the world may be expected to arise out of the present exertions of the Spaniard, is a sentiment worthy of lines less humdrum, & common-place than those in which you have at present dressed it.[19]

One senses a suppressed resentment of the gifted younger brother, whose last poem, *Palestine*, had scored such a notable triumph.

Heber's second great interest was Continental literature, particularly romances like *Amadis de Gaul* and their translations into various European languages, including English. The most valuable book in the Heber sale, according to Dibdin, was the first edition of the Spanish romance *Tirant lo Blanc* (Valencia 1490), for which Heber paid 300 guineas at the Rich sale in 1826, and which sold in 1835 for £105.[20] The Continental and classical bias of the collection is illustrated by a brief schedule of the library at Hodnet that Heber drew up in August 1811. At that date, the two largest single categories in a library of 9000 volumes were French books, with 1800 volumes, and Italian books (1100 in all). There was a much smaller collection of Spanish and Portuguese books, soon to be greatly augmented at the Stanley sale in 1813. The combined categories of Greek and Latin classics came to about 1300 volumes, and modern Latin books, including history, poetry and philology, to about 1700. This is a reminder that Heber's collection of English literature needs to be placed in the context of the collection as a whole, just as his copy of *The History of Jason* (Caxton, Westminster 1477) stands in his sale catalogue alongside French and Dutch versions of the same romance, *L'Histoire de Palmerin d'Olive* (Paris 1549) alongside *Palmerin d'Oliva, the Mirrour of Nobilitie* (London 1588-97), and *Palmerin of England* (London 1602) alongside *Palmerin d'Inglaterra* (Toledo 1547-8).[21]

The English literature was, however, the most expensive and most prized part of Heber's collection, its special status indicated by its separation from the rest of the library, in 'one very small room, situated on the ground floor' of his house in Pimlico.[22] Heber was passionately interested in English drama, not just as a reader but as a spectator. His pocket diaries record frequent visits to the theatre, with a predictable liking for Shakespeare (Kemble's performance as Shylock in *The Merchant of Venice* at Drury Lane in December 1797 is singled out for special mention) and a more unexpected taste for Gothic melodramas like *The Haunted Tower*, which he saw twice at Drury Lane in 1791.[23] It would be interesting to know if Heber perceived any disparity between his collection of the classics and his collection of popular literature, or whether his interest in English poetry and drama was recreational rather than academic. The answer is probably no. One commentator on Heber's library remarked that it was designed to illustrate one theme in particular, 'the origin of romantic literature . . . the discussion of which has engaged the pens of so many elegant authors of the last and present centuries'; and the collection effectively defines (partly by exclusion: Heber collected French and Italian literature much more thoroughly than German or Dutch) a literary canon that runs from the Greek and Latin classics, through the romance literature of the Middle Ages and Renaissance, to the English literature of the last three centuries.

This was by no means the full extent of Heber's collections. He also owned a fine collection of coins, concentrating on Greek and Roman coins and Renaissance portrait medals; a large number of illustrated books and prints, including all the most important works of eighteenth-century architecture and classical archaeology; a small but carefully chosen group of Italian Old Master prints and drawings, particularly strong in the works of the engraver Marc Antonio; and a collection of paintings, mostly English historical portraits but with a few modern works, notably a self-portrait of Angelica Kauffman for which Heber paid two guineas at the Roscoe sale in 1816 and which sold for nine shillings at his own sale in 1834.[24] But by Heber's time this style of collecting was beginning to seem slightly old-fashioned. The art collectors of the early nineteenth century tended to be professional men — artists, architects or apostles of neo-classical taste like John Soane, Richard Payne Knight and Thomas Hope — rather than gentlemen of leisure like Heber, and classical antiquity and fine art were in any case passing from the private cabinet to the public gallery. 'Mr Heber is buying *Marc-Antonios* at the sale of Seratti's prints!' wrote Dibdin to Lord Spencer in 1816, clearly regarding this as the latest manifestation of Heber's eccentricity. 'I suppose, in due time, he will attack *Finiguerra-sculptures!*'[25] Books, similarly, tended to be collected in isolation, as objects of literary rather than aesthetic significance. The new style of collecting was represented by Thomas Grenville, who discarded a

Finiguerra engraving from his library 'deeming it', his nephew the Duke of Buckingham explained to Dibdin, 'as more properly belonging to a classical collection of prints than to his library, which does not include any collection of that description.'[26] Moreover, rising prices made it increasingly difficult to collect art and antiquities as well as books. Heber told Dibdin in 1815 that he was 'well pleased with his book-purchases this season, but that the Greek Coins brought frightful prices.'[27] In attempting to collect on both fronts, Heber was behind the times: an eighteenth-century virtuoso rather than a nineteenth-century scholar-collector.

In *Taste and Technique in Book Collecting*, John Carter comes to the opposite conclusion. He maintains that Heber was ahead of his times, and that while his aristocratic contemporaries collected books in a few selected fields — *editiones principes*, Aldines, Elsevirs — in fine bindings and superlative condition, Heber took a scholar's rather than a connoisseur's interest in his books, collecting widely in neglected areas of literature and history and paying less attention to condition.[28] There is an element of truth in this: it explains, for example, why the Heber sale catalogues disappointed many observers. 'I suppose there *will* be some fine Heber sales!' wrote Henry Drury rather dubiously to Dibdin in September 1834. 'Drama excepted, dull work as yet.'[29] Dibdin remarked that 'the condition of the books, generally speaking, was far from *tempting*'. Heber once told him that he could easily have spent another £5000 on rebinding his books; Dibdin remarked cattily that it would have been money well spent.[30] But one should not exaggerate the difference between Heber and his contemporaries. For one thing, his main collecting interests — the Greek and Latin classics, French, Spanish and Italian romances, early English literature — were not at all unusual by the standards of the day. Nor was he indifferent to the condition of his books. Alexander Dyce, indeed, remembered him as a fastidious collector: ' "Look," Richard Heber would say in a melancholy tone, "only look at this volume which Porson has just returned to me! When I lent it to him, it was quite spotless, and now it is perfectly beastly." '[31] His more valuable books were frequently rebound in morocco, in the discreetly elegant style favoured by collectors of the period, with gilt edges and a modicum of ornamentation on the boards. Charles Lewis was his preferred binder: Dibdin noted in 1812 that Lewis, who 'is really a most able artist ... has been binding about 150 volumes for Mr Heber, in a stile of elegance, surpassing everything I ever saw', and observed after Heber's death that he had 'of late years . . . expended hundreds – if not thousands – with Lewis' in a rebinding programme for the books at Pimlico.[32]

In many ways Heber's attitude to condition was typical of his time. His attention to detail in binding, as well as his indifference to original condition, are summed up in a letter to a fellow-collector in March 1813 advising him on the binding of a volume of tracts: 'I shd. recommend you, without loss of time, to put it into the hands of some experienced binder, with a strict charge to stiffen the whole well with the strongest size, (leaf by leaf) after which it will bear handling, & each tract may be bound separate, & the most valuable mended with care previous to binding.'[33] He had no qualms about perfecting a book from several imperfect copies. His copy of *The Boke of Comfort* (1525), the first English translation of Boethius to appear in print, is described in his sale catalogue as 'fine copy, in morocco' and has a long note by Heber: 'I purchased it at the Sale of Mr Richard Foster, Nov. 1806, for 7*l*. 17*s*. 6*d*. ill-bound in russia, gilt leaves. It then wanted 18 leaves . . . I afterwards completed it from another imperfect copy (formerly Ratcliffe's) which was bought by Gough for 2*l*. 6*s*. in 1776, and by me at Gough's Sale for 14*l*. 3*s*. 6*d*. and had it then bound by Lewis.'[34] The common-or-garden eighteenth-century books that made up the bulk of Heber's library received less attention from the binder: his copy of a volume of light verse, *Modern Midnight Conversation*, one of the relatively few eighteenth-century books that Heber had rebound, was given to the binder James Rodwell to put into a plain calf binding at a cost of ninepence.[35] Books like these, inexpensive modern books in drab bindings, were what Dibdin and Drury felt lowered the tone of Heber's library. STC, incidentally, records six copies of *The Boke of Comfort*, and ESTC records three copies of *Modern Midnight Conversation*, not including Heber's own. In terms of rarity there is not a lot to choose between them, and Heber deserves to be saluted for recognizing the intrinsic interest and imminent scarcity of many unregarded eighteenth-century books. But we can tell from their bindings that the modern books occupied a fairly low status in the social hierarchy of Heber's library, and we should not really expect otherwise.

Apart from his distaste for large-paper copies on the grounds that they took up too much space,[36] Heber's attitude to binding and condition was not very different from that of his Roxburghe Club contemporaries. In one respect, however, he stands out as highly unusual: he had no bookplate, and no armorial bookstamp. The most familiar sign of Heber's ownership is the rectangular ink-stamp on the flyleaves of many of his books; the stamp that gives this paper its title, and that received a marvellously barbed compliment from John Carter: 'No bibliophile', wrote Carter, 'can look unmoved on the small black oblong stamp of the BIBLIOTHECA HEBERIANA, however warmly he may deplore library stamps as a substitute for signatures and however mediocre may be the condition of the book in which this one is found.[37] As far as I can tell, however, the title 'Bibliotheca Heberiana' was coined by Dibdin after Heber's death, and the bookstamp seems to have been added at that stage as a way of marking the property in the saleroom to prevent theft. In some volumes the bookstamp is smudged, as though added in a hurry, or even printed upside-down; in others it does not appear at all, and the only mark of Heber's ownership is his note of the date, price and place of purchase, in the top right-hand corner of the first flyleaf. Heber very rarely put his name to a book: the only books to carry his signature are his very earliest acquisitions and a few later purchases that he may have lent to friends. In this respect he was one of the most self-effacing collectors of his generation.

It may seem odd to describe Heber as self-effacing when he was such a visible presence in the auction rooms. As a rule he seems to have sat right at the front, beside the rostrum: one eyewitness account of the Roxburghe sale has him sitting 'close at the auctioneer's back most busily employ'd' and the story goes that when he wished to bid without attracting attention, he used to signal his bids by treading on the auctioneer's toes. According to Heber's obituary in the *Morning Chronicle*, the auctioneer George Leigh 'used to complain bitterly, and look unutterable anguish, occasioned by treads on the toe, pluckings and thumps on the back and shoulders, and other silent practical indications given him by Heber, when he wished to conceal his biddings from his opponent, who was often his friend.'[38] Heber was aware that he was an object of close scrutiny in the auction room, and some accounts imply that he rather relished the attention. 'When last in Town,' wrote Dawson Turner in May 1825, 'I had frequently the pleasure of seeing Mr Heber, but never so much in his glory as at the sale of Rhodes' library at Sotheby's, whence he marched one day in high feather with a dirty, ill-looking old play under his arm, for which I think I understood him he had given 27 Guineas.'[39] But he was also capable of elaborate mystification in order to conceal his activities. He 'never appeared to be emulous of reaching notice as a book collector', recalled the *Morning Chronicle*. 'We have known him to entrust his commissions to four different persons on the same day and in the same sale, himself, the fifth, being likewise present.'[40]

There are several reasons why Heber might have wished to remain anonymous. Private collectors who bid in person were sometimes the object of hostility from members of the trade (notably at the Lort sale in 1791), and the same obituary notice of Heber records that he 'experienced many annoyances at the auctions from the booksellers, whom in his early initiation he constantly opposed'.[41] 'All the Booksellers', wrote Daniel Terry after attending the Roxburghe sale, 'complain of the impossibility of purchasing anything out of the hands of gentleman-collectors.'[42] Another good reason for anonymity was that Heber was often bidding against his friends, much to their frustration. 'I am sure of losing all my commissions' lamented Dibdin when he heard that Heber was likely to be present at a sale. 'In contending with Heber,' wrote George Chalmers ruefully, 'I have a hard antagonist.'[43] Yet Heber went to such lengths to conceal his identity that one suspects something more was involved, and that, as I have already suggested, he was motivated not just by practical considerations but by a love of secrecy for its own sake. 'Heber's mode of bidding at auctions was perpetually varied', recalled his obituarist. 'We have frequently seen him bid against himself, or rather against the person whom he had commissioned to buy the book, in order to delude the bystanders.'[44]

As a result, it is very difficult to reconstruct Heber's purchases at auction. For example, marked copies of the catalogue of the Gordonstoun library, an important collection of seventeenth-century books sold by J. G. Cochrane in 1816, record the collector J. D. Phelps as the purchaser of some of the most valuable items. In fact Phelps was bidding on Heber's behalf: 'If you bid,' Heber wrote to him, 'pray put down all articles which *exceed* £5 to your own name, at the end of the sale—you can explain the matter to Cochrane charging him however to be secret. The rest may be entered in my own name—& all charged on one bill.[45] Without other evidence, such as an invoice, we should be very wary of assuming that the lots marked down to 'Heber' in any given sale catalogue represent the full extent of his purchases. In many cases, according to the *Morning Chronicle*, the auctioneer simply put the book in his desk 'and placed in his catalogue as the purchaser such a *nom de guerre* as might occur to him at the moment'. There is the further complication that Heber often gave his commissions to booksellers. At one stage in his career he used Robert Triphook as his agent. One of his letters to Triphook, giving him commissions for a forthcoming sale, has survived and shows how much he relied on Triphook's judgement. 'If good copies, a fair price', writes Heber against one lot, and again, 'If clean, a few shillings, but use your discretion'. He adds: 'You will buy them in your own name.'[46]

Triphook was a talented but unscrupulous individual, and from a remark made by Dibdin in 1819 ('Heber has even *bought of Triphook!*') it appears that the two had not parted company on the best of terms.[47] At any rate, Heber's agent for the last 20 years of his life was the bookseller Thomas Thorpe. Thorpe may have lacked Triphook's polish, but he was a compulsive book buyer, who went on buying even at his own bankruptcy sale, in whom Heber perhaps recognized a kindred spirit. He paid Thorpe 15% commission, described by one contemporary as 'the regular and understood commission charged by booksellers to gentlemen'. The usual rate, then as now, was 10%, but as Thorpe's most favoured customer Heber had nothing to complain about.[48] He had the first refusal of any item in Thorpe's stock, often to the disadvantage of other customers: 'I think I told you', wrote Thorpe to Heber in 1826, 'the Advocates are quite pleased with their purchase of the Astorga collection, I hope no one will know you had picked them, as tho I sold only such as in catalogue [*sic*] I am rather unpleasantly situated in my own feelings not having told them you had some of them'. If other collectors wanted Thorpe to bid for them they had to leave their commissions, as he explained to Heber, 'with the understanding of them not interfering with yours'.[49] Heber's relationship with Thorpe illustrates what might be called the professionalization of the book trade. Gentlemen no longer bid in person at auction sales but relied on their agent to bid on their behalf. There is a telling moment in 1827 when Thorpe apologizes to Heber for not sending him the latest auction catalogues in time for the sale, and complains that the auctioneers 'get into such a horrid way of the Catalogue out one day and sell the next or day after that'.[50] The era of bibliomania, of high prices and high-profile sales, was coming to an end. It was becoming increasingly difficult for private individuals, particularly those living outside London, to get hold of sale catalogues, let alone view the books; and if they wished to form a collection they needed a professional to watch the market for them.

The large quantity of rare books flooding on to the market in the early nineteenth century, together with the relatively small number of private collectors, created a buyers' market and put Heber in a very powerful position. As early as 1815 George Chalmers predicted that prices would start to fall as the leading collectors filled the gaps in their libraries: 'There are only about 5 leading Collectors of old Romances and as they are all nearly full this class of books have fallen very greatly in value. The Collectors of Old English Poetry are much more numerous but the leading & most extravagant ones have got pretty full, & the numerous reprints have supplied much of what was wanting.'[51] To lose Heber's custom, Thorpe declared in 1826, 'would be to me one of the greatest disasters that could occur'; and after Heber's death in 1833 it was claimed that his absence from the market had caused prices to fall by a third.[52] With a reputation like this, it is hardly surprising that Heber was able to establish an ascendancy over the trade. Writing to the Edinburgh bookseller William Blackwood with an order from his latest catalogue, Heber confidently expected to be given priority: 'Those which I have marked with a *cross* prefixed, I feel *particularly* desirous of, [and] if there should be any other orders—would thank you for the preference'.[53]

Heber's true impact on the market is harder to gauge. At the Dampier sale in 1813 he spent just over £73, roughly 6% of the total, and at the Gordonstoun sale in 1816 he spent £160, about 10% of the total.[54] These figures, of course, fail to take into account his role as an underbidder, but from his list of commissions for the second half of the Gordonstoun sale it appears that while he left low bids on a good many items, he was underbidder on relatively few. His order from Blackwood's catalogue amounted to something over £32, a substantial amount but by no means the largest order Blackwood received; Thomas Grenville, for instance, ordered approximately £87, and Triphook, on behalf of the Marquess of Blandford, £89 worth of books. The impression one receives from these figures is that Heber bought steadily but not regardless of cost, and did not dominate the bidding (or, perhaps, the book trade) in the way that richer collectors were able to do. At the Roxburghe sale, Thomas Park noted that Heber was 'almost beaten out of the circle by the pugilistic force of heavier purses', and Heber's own commentary on the sale conveys a sense of detachment from the excesses of the bibliomania:

The prices at which the articles of rarity especially in the Poetical & Romance departments have sold in this collection have exceeded all expectation, precedent, or credibility—owing in a great measure to the sudden appearance of two noblemen in the market—the one a young Duke [Devonshire], rich & sanguine, the other a Marquis [Blandford], long engaged in the pursuit but newly refreshed by a seasonable supply from Blenheim. These 2 were the great competitors—& their effect on the market could not but be sensibly experienced.[55]

When prices were high, Heber let the books go and waited for cheaper copies. At the Roxburghe sale the First Folio of Shakespeare sold for £100; Heber waited 20 years before buying a copy for £51 at the Broadley sale in 1832, only a year before his death.

Heber also carried out several commissions at the Roxburghe sale on behalf of his friends. For Walter Scott he bought a number of early French romances, including *L'Hystoire de Guerin de Montglave* for £3.1.0 and *Les Faits et Gestes de Huon de Bourdeaulx* (1516) for £20.5.0. 'I begged off all the great collectors in your name,' he told Scott, 'and succeeded for 6141 the Montglave otherwise you would have paid in the same proportion for that—for the Huon de Bourdeaux I tried to do the same—but a man in buckram, whom I did not know, spoiled all. However, I did not like losing, what you seemed to wish for so much—especially as you may put it in the advocates Library, when you tire of it. The other romances went as high, in many cases, & in some much higher.'[56] This episode is interesting for what it tells us about Heber's sense of social propriety. He was willing to bargain with other collectors, and his friendship with Lord Spencer, to whom he sold a number of books, did not prevent him from driving some very hard bargains indeed.[57] Bargaining with booksellers, however, was a different matter. Unlike Sir Thomas Phillipps, Heber always paid the marked price ('Taking discount will do once', he is supposed to have said, 'but it will not do a second time'[58]) and never demanded favourable commission rates. The distinction is neatly summed up in a letter to Triphook asking him to find out the buyer of a lot that Heber was particularly anxious to obtain: 'if a bookseller *buy* it;' writes Heber, 'if a gentleman, let me know his name by return of post'. Booksellers did business with booksellers; gentlemen did business with gentlemen.

But to return to the question with which we began: what was the use of Heber's collection? What did he do with his books? Here we encounter an embarrassing silence. Except for the edition of Silius

Italicus which he edited as a first-year undergraduate in 1792, and leaving aside the unpublished editions of Persius and Claudian which he prepared about the same time, Heber published nothing under his own name. Despite being one of the founders of the *Quarterly Review*, he never wrote for the journal. The one and only book he presented to the Roxburghe Club, a reprint of Cutwode's *Caltha Poetarum*, contains no preface, no notes, and no scholarly apparatus of any kind. Perhaps this should not surprise us: it is, after all, entirely consistent with the man whose self-effacing, secretive character I have already sketched, who hardly ever wrote his name in his books, and who sat in Parliament for five years without ever opening his mouth. But his reticence perplexed his contemporaries—his silence in Parliament was, we are told, 'considered as remarkable by his friends, from his known powers and the fluency of his private conversation'—and some attempt to explain it is called for here.[59]

Walter Scott, who knew both brothers, once remarked that Reginald Heber suffered, as a poet, from 'a too easy situation in life'. A man who wants to achieve literary distinction 'is compelled', wrote Scott, no doubt reflecting on his own case, 'to place himself frequently before the public. But the man of affluence naturally shrinks from the trouble necessary to assert his literary rank, and from exposing himself to virulent criticism and unnecessary cabal.'[60] This makes equally good sense as an explanation of Richard Heber's reluctance to go into print. But the truth may be that Heber simply lacked the stamina and the application to produce a work of scholarship. There were some sorts of research he undoubtedly did enjoy: collating his books, checking them against published descriptions in Panzer or Mattaire, and finally writing the neat little note 'c & p' on the flyleaf; going through old sale catalogues, tracing the provenance of a particular copy or locating a previously unrecorded edition; drawing up catalogues of parts of his collection, and marking the entries 'G', 'V.G.' or 'Fine' according to condition. Dibdin reported to Spencer in September 1812 that Heber was spending his time 'collating his Roxburgh purchases—from 6 in the Morning, till 10 at night'.[61] But the purpose of all this collation was simply to ensure that the books were perfect. Heber seems to have had little interest in other forms of bibliographical inquiry, such as analysing a book's typography in order to identify its printer and date, and his surviving bibliographical notes are rather a sad show, half-finished lists of books that peter out after a few pages. He told Sir Thomas Phillipps in 1829 that he intended 'to commence a catalogue of his books, by taking a portion of them at a time, as 1 the Class of History, 2 Romances, 3 Theology &c &c &c.' Predictably enough, it was never completed.

Heber's real talent was as midwife to other people's books. Arguably his greatest service to literature was the encouragement he gave to Walter Scott at the beginning of his career. He attempted, without success, to use his influence to get Scott's early play *The House of Aspen* performed at Drury Lane, and urged Scott to persevere with his other literary projects: 'By the bye,' he wrote to Scott in 1800, 'how goes on the collection of tales of wonder — it seems to me to hang fire — I want to see you in print that I may "join the shout of unsuspected praise". And pray do not forget your promise to set out the border anecdotes — on which I reckon much.'[62] Heber also supervised the publication of his brother Reginald's poetry, and any student of publishing history in search of a dissertation topic could do worse than look at Richard's letters to Reginald, which are full of bibliographical detail and show what a close and informed interest he took in the business of publishing and the appearance of books. When he wrote to Reginald in March 1809 to advise him of the imminent publication of his poem *Europe*, he warned him: 'As to emoluments, I would not have you very sanguine. Out of a 2s pamphlet, no great profits can be drawn, & in making it 2s. Hatchard thinks I overdid it — however, I instructed him to put a neat stained paper wrapper over the outside, by way of giving it a more imposing exterior than a common pamphlet, & so got him to consent to the extra 6d.'[63] It was entirely characteristic of Heber to prefer a high price and a limited print run. 'Europe has reached a second Edition', he wrote three months later, 'which however I limited to 500 Copies not wishing to make your labours too common, or throw pearls before swine.'[64] Here, perhaps, we have part of the explanation for Heber's own reluctance to publish.

In George Ellis's *Specimens of the Early English Poets*, a pioneering anthology of sixteenth- and seventeenth-century English poetry, we have a unique example of Heber's not only seeing a book through the press but making use of his collections in order to do so. Heber's copy of the first edition of 1790, with his notes towards the second edition of 1801, is now in the Folger Library.[65] His notes transform a textual shambles into something approaching modern standards of accuracy: he collates the texts against the original editions, where possible against more than one (Gascoigne's poems against the editions of 1572 and 1575, Davison's poems against the editions of 1602, 1611 and 1621), and is punctilious about recording omissions, 'which should always I think be acknowledged,' he told Ellis, '& may be expressed in printing by a few small stars, without materially injuring the beauty of the page'. Heber's familiarity with seventeenth-century poetry also leads him to make a number of suggestions for enlarging the anthology, some of which seem remarkably prescient: for example, he suggests several poems by John Donne to augment the two extracts printed by Ellis. Heber and his friend Thomas Park supervised the publication of the third edition of the book, where several of these suggestions are included.[66] This is the only example I know of Heber himself editing the books he owned, but there are plenty of examples of his lending books to other scholars for use in editions or anthologies of a similar sort. A letter to David Laing in 1820, accompanying the loan of a volume of poetry, is interesting for the conditions that Heber attaches to the loan. 'You will oblige me', he writes, 'by not suffering the little Volume to go out of your own hands, more especially into those of a *printer*, tho you are at full liberty to make any extracts you may judge suitable to your purpose ... You will observe the title-page is extremely *tender*, & requires, as well as the rest of the little Volume to be *gently* handled.'[67] Was Heber afraid of an unauthorized, textually corrupt edition, or did he simply fear for the book's safety in the hands of a printer?

Heber was a sociable man, fully aware of the social utility of his collections. The giving and receiving of books, the exchange of small scholarly favours, all formed part of the social cement that brought Heber and his friends together. This is strikingly illustrated in his letters to one of his closest Oxford friends, Dr Martin Routh, President of Magdalen College.[68] Heber executed Routh's commissions at auction sales, used his scholarly connections on the Continent to acquire a collation of a manuscript in Paris that Routh needed for his *Reliquiae Sacrae*, negotiated with Routh's London publisher when the book came out, and saw to the binding of the presentation copies. In return, Routh protected Heber's political interests in Oxford over a period of fifteen years, from 1806, when Heber stood unsuccessfully for Parliament, to 1821, when he was finally elected as MP for the University. It was the custom of the University that prospective candidates did not declare themselves but allowed themselves to be nominated, did not canvass for votes in person but permitted their friends to do so on their behalf, and did not show themselves in Oxford during the election. Heber was thus wholly dependent on the efforts of friends like Routh in mobilizing the Tory vote; as his election manager wrote proudly in 1806, the voting figures were a 'testimony . . . to the world of what personal influence can do'.[69] As the saying goes, the personal is political, and as Heber's correspondence with Routh demonstrates, the bibliographical could be political too. His position in the bibliographical world secured him the influential support of Dibdin's patron, the Whig magnate Lord Spencer. 'Heber is of very different politics from me', wrote Spencer during the 1821 election, but all the same 'I am very eager for Mr Heber's success'.[70]

I have left the most important question till last: how much did Heber actually spend on his books? Dibdin estimated the total cost at £150,000; later he revised his estimate to £100,000, 'but', he added, 'I know of nothing certain upon the subject beyond *this* — that whether it were 150,000*l.* or 100,000*l.* it was an IMMENSE SUM.' In estimating Heber's annual expenditure we are on slightly firmer ground. Writing to Dawson Turner in 1833, Edward Magrath claimed that 'in the year 1827 Mr Hodsall who was then his Banker informed me that for the 20 years preceding he had annually paid £5,000 on account of Books purchased by Mr Heber.' Dibdin, who had seen the bank books, came up with a similar figure: 'For 20 years he spent from 5 to 7000£ per annum in books — and in *one* of those 20 years (1824) not less than *£9700*.'[71] Without an accurate estimate of Heber's annual income it is hard to place this in context, but it undoubtedly represented a perilously high level of expenditure.

At first, Heber's expenditure on books was treated as one of the comical aspects of his character. In 1813, when an unrecorded Caxton was rumoured to be at large, Dibdin wrote facetiously to Spencer that 'Mr Heber would sell his whole Yorkshire property for a copy of it'. Heber himself joined in the joke: 'It is but another rick or two', he is reported to have said when buying a particularly expensive book.[72] But by the 1820s the joke was becoming less amusing. When Heber was standing for Parliament in 1821, Dibdin saw him in the auction room and fretted about his extravagance:

There are some very extraordinary books selling at Sotheby's. Heber was there yesterday — and would stop (against the remonstrance of Mr Wynn) to see the Spanish Romances sell — for *£120*: he is thought to be the purchaser, though bought in the name of Thorpe. I wish, just now, he would leave the dead for the living. Again:– people now begin to speak out about his *manner* of *living* &c: this will give his rival a powerful advantage over him.

In the same year Heber mortgaged some of his Shropshire estates for £9000. This kept him solvent for a few more years, but saddled him with a new debt which he had difficulty in paying off: his friend James Stanhope, one of the lenders, complained that 'you are indeed so unpunctual in the payment of the mortgage that you expose me every other year to the greatest inconvenience'.[73]

This is the background to an extraordinary letter that Heber wrote to his brother Reginald in January 1823. Reginald had just accepted the bishopric of Calcutta, thereby vacating the family living of Hodnet, and Richard was writing to inform him of 'the individual, whom . . . I propose as your successor. This, you will, perhaps, be surprized, when you find to be no other than *myself.*'

In truth, I feel my old inclination to become the Pastor of Hodnet revive: my Parliamentary duties, as far as my experience extends, are rather irksome than inviting, & I suspect that I should pass my time more agreeably among my neighbours, my books, & my trees at Hodnet, than amidst the bad air, & bad blood, of St Stephen's Chapel. Add to this the change in the times. You know, as well as I can tell you, Rents have already fallen considerably, & must yet fall more. Land bought, with borrowed money, in dear times, begins to tell unpleasant tales, & I have no scruple in saying that the difference of income produced by the addition of Hodnet Rectory, (deteriorated as it is) is far from being a fact unworthy of consideration.[74]

For a sitting MP to resign his seat, become an ordained minister in the Church of England and present himself to a family living worth £2000 a year would not have seemed as questionable by the standards of the 1820s as it appears to us now, but even so, it was a considerable step to take and graphically reveals the extent of Heber's financial plight. 'I sincerely regret that you have so far felt the pressure of the times as to make such an increase of your income desirable', wrote Reginald in reply. But when Heber went abroad in July 1825 the living of Hodnet was still vacant, and when he resigned his seat in January 1826 he did not have a peaceful country retirement to look forward to, but five years of exile on the Continent.

I have written elsewhere of Heber's flight to the Continent and his refusal, against the advice of all his friends, to return to England. In the light of that remarkable letter to Reginald it seems likely that his financial affairs were reaching a crisis at the time of his departure. But his position as an MP gave him some protection against his creditors, and there seems little doubt that he left England as a result of allegations of homosexual practices that might have led to criminal prosecution.[75] The full story will probably never be known. Heber's behaviour was the subject of all sorts of rumours, most of them pure speculation: it was alleged that a warrant for his arrest had actually been issued when he left the country, and Dibdin was shown a copy of a letter supposedly from Heber on the subject of 'young women & boys' which he pronounced to be a forgery. Heber's own reaction was to take no notice of the allegations: 'I shall proceed as if nothing had happened, and shall come home in my own good time, whether it be sooner or later.' Disregard of public opinion and concealment of private feelings were both perfectly in character. But some speculation is permissible: as a book collector, it is possible that Heber was aware of pamphlets published during the French Revolution arguing that sexual behaviour was the responsibility of individuals, not of the state, and therefore a private matter; as a classicist, he would have been aware of the existence and tolerance of homosexuality in classical society, and would probably have known recent scholarship on the subject, such as Richard Payne Knight's *Discourse upon the Worship of Priapus*, with its bold speculations about the sexual origins of Greek and Roman religion. Heber was acquainted with Knight, who presented him with a copy of his *Prolegomena in Homerum* in 1808.[76] Did his knowledge of the sexual ethics of the classical world provide him with a justification of his own sexual orientation? Heber's statement, in a letter to Dibdin, that he had 'a conscience void of offence' can be interpreted either as a formal profession of innocence, or as a more ambiguous declaration that he was conscious of no wrongdoing.

While on the Continent, Heber continued to collect books. In March 1829 Sir Thomas Phillipps encountered him in Paris: 'Met Mr Heber at Silvester's Auction Rooms', he recorded in a notebook. 'He entered into conversation with me, by recommending me not to buy a book which I was bidding for, because it was imperfect. He is called Mr Richard by the auctioneers.' The two collectors discussed recent sales of manuscripts, and Heber marked the occasion, as we learn from Phillipps's annotated copy of the catalogue, by buying a volume of 50 early sixteenth-century Italian poetical tracts for 1260 francs.[77] Other reports of Heber filtered back to England from time to time. In 1830 the bookseller John Payne met Heber in Louvain and found him 'as gay, chatty, & amusing as ever!' as Dibdin told Lord Spencer:

He lately made a most extraordinary haul of *Irish Historical* books—from the neighbouring Convent of *Tongerlou*: books (he says) of which Mr Grenville never heard of the *Titles*: (This, perhaps a little maliciously, I mentioned to Mr Grenville yesterday—and the intelligence evidently produced a *sensation.*)

Heber's book depositories in Paris, Ghent, Brussels, Antwerp and Frankfurt date from this period. It is clear from the Paris and Ghent sale catalogues of his library that most of the books were recent purchases: the Ghent catalogue mentions items from the Bollandists' library, sold in 1825, the Lauwers collection, sold in 1829, and the abbey of Parck, sold in 1830. Heber's purchases from the Continent before 1825 were less extensive than one might imagine. He complained to Routh in 1811 that 'the expences of insurance, freight, duty &c. added to the unfavourable state of exchange, tend to augment the price of foreign purchases to an enormous degree.'[78]

Heber's financial affairs continued to cause concern. His friend John Richardson wrote to him in February 1826, soon after Heber's resignation from Parliament became known, to inform him of 'the rumours, which are current here, about the supposed extent of your pecuniary difficulties'. Heber owed Richardson the sum of £2300, plus two years' unpaid interest, and Richardson considered that, as a personal friend, he should have priority over Heber's other creditors.

If your engagements exceed, as I fear they must, what your income can speedily satisfy, why should you not make up your mind to raise at once by mortgage or sale a sufficient sum to satisfy every body & particularly to satisfy yourself by placing you at ease? I have spoken throughout with the frankness of old friendship, which I know you will understand & approve.[79]

Richardson was mollified to discover that Heber intended to mortgage his Norfolk estates to pay his debts. 'I have never, I assure you, at all doubted that your intentions towards me were quite honorable,' he promised Heber in 1828, 'tho I admit I may have entertained some doubts of your promptitude and decision in matters of business of this kind.' But as months passed with no word from Heber, Richardson began to panic, and in December 1829, on hearing that Heber's creditors were taking legal proceedings against him which would render his estate liable to forfeiture, he wrote to Heber bitterly reproaching him for his 'extraordinary irresolution and procrastination'. In June 1830 Heber finally bowed to the inevitable and mortgaged his house and estates in Hodnet for the sum of £40,000, £10,000 of which was used to pay off the earlier mortgage of 1821.[80]

Having settled his debts, Heber returned to England in the summer of 1831. The mortgage of Hodnet gave him the money to buy books on an extensive scale, and some of his most important purchases were made in the 1830s, including part of the Daniel collection of Elizabethan ballads, which he bought from Thorpe for £273 in 1832. In other respects his life after 1830 was a sad one. 'Into society he can never hope to be again admitted,' wrote Alexander Dyce to John Payne Collier in August 1831, 'I mean, even if he were guiltless, which his returning leads one to suppose; there will always be "a something" about him, which people can't easily forget.'[81] Whether or not to recognize Heber constituted a ticklish social problem in the London salerooms and clubrooms of the 1830s. 'The Duke of Devonshire told me', wrote Dibdin, 'that, for his part, if he *met* him, he should certainly *speak* to him — as nothing seemed to be substantiated against him.' Dawson Turner was not so confident. 'To my great comfort,' he told Dibdin after Heber's death, 'I never saw him afterwards; had we met, I was resolved to go up to him directly & offer him my hand; but', he added with relief, 'I was spared the necessity'. It is not surprising to read in Heber's obituary that 'with the exception of his visits to the auction-rooms and booksellers' shops' he lived 'entirely secluded among his books at Pimlico or Hodnet'. In October 1833 he died at Pimlico, of 'an oppression in his breathing, & palpitation at the heart', according to his sister, leading to a heart attack 'aggravated probably by mental anxiety', according to popular gossip, '& habits of excessive drinking'.[82]

Probably Heber's library had never been in perfect order. As early as 1820 there is a letter from Heber to Lackington's the booksellers, apologizing for returning an unwanted book four years after it had been received, and explaining that the parcel 'had till then remained unexamined'.[83] But it was only later in the 1820s, with Heber absent on the Continent, that the situation really got out of hand, as books piled up in his London lodgings with no one to arrange them. In his *Reminiscences* Dibdin has given us a graphic account of the chaos at Pimlico after Heber's death:

I looked around me with amazement. I had never seen rooms, cupboards, passages, and corridors, so choked, so suffocated with books. Treble rows were here, double rows were there. Hundreds of slim quartos — several upon each other—were longitudinally placed over thin and stunted duodecimos, reaching from one extremity of a shelf to another. Up to the very ceiling the piles of *volumes* extended; while the floor was strewed with them, in loose and numerous heaps. When I looked on all *this*, and thought what might be at *Hodnet*, and upon the *Continent*, it were difficult to describe my emotions. 'Vox faucibus haesit!'[84]

In all this confusion Heber's will was nowhere to be found. 'Drawers without number, and boxes without end,' writes Dibdin, 'were emptied of their contents. Bills, notes, memoranda, letters, communications of every kind and description—but still NO WILL.' His letters to Lord Spencer during this period, now in the Althorp papers at Northampton, paint a vivid picture of the scene at Pimlico, with the floors uncarpeted, the servants wandering around aimlessly, and books 'strewn on the floor, like the leaves of a forest! Nor will it be deem'd marvellous:- when the marriage settlement of his Father & Mother (upon which the title of the Norfolk estates is founded) was pick'd up lying on the floor!!—Yesterday I found the *probate of his Father's will* in the like situation!—and I feel perfectly persuaded that his *own will*—after all—will be found stuff'd within the *covers* of a *book*. Meanwhile, the lawyer is gone to *Leyden*—the searches at *Paris* being quite fruitless.'[85]

In January 1834, three months after Heber's death, Dibdin finally found the will tucked behind some books on an upper shelf at Pimlico. The discovery was not quite as dramatic as he makes it appear in his *Reminiscences*, since the contents of the will were already known from a copy provided by Heber's friend Henry Hobhouse. Dibdin is correct, strictly speaking, to say that the will made no mention of the books, but the wording of the will makes it quite clear that Heber intended the library to be sold. His sister Mary was made sole executrix, with instructions to 'dispose of my personal property to the best advantage and apply it in liquidation of my just debts' and to sell the Norfolk, Suffolk and Yorkshire estates if this should prove insufficient.[86] The mortgage on the Hodnet estate made it imperative to sell the library as quickly as possible, and it was dispersed in a series of sales at London, Oxford, Paris and Ghent, beginning in April 1834, less than three months after probate.[87]

John Carter sums Heber up as 'an omnivorous reader, a great scholar, a passionate collector'. He was all of those things, but it would be misleading to categorize him as a scholar-collector in the sense of someone who collected books for use in his own scholarly projects. His books, coins, paintings and prints were essentially an expression of his taste, not a collection of research materials, and this is surely why he never felt the need to produce scholarly work of his own. Heber was that quintessentially eighteenth-century figure, the dilettante, for whom the title of scholar-collector would be an anachronism. But even though he was one of the heroes of Dibdin's *Bibliomania*, the textbook of book collecting as private gratification, Heber's library had an important public function. His justification for collecting duplicates has become famous: 'Why, you see, Sir, no man can comfortably do without three copies of a book. One he must have for his show copy, and he will probably keep it at his country house. Another he will require for his own use and reference; and unless he is inclined to part with this, which is very inconvenient, or risk the injury of his best copy, he must needs have a third at the service of his friends.'[88] Ludicrous overkill? Perhaps; but it also encapsulates the dual aspects, private and public, of Heber's collecting. From the very beginning of his career he sought out the company of scholars and put his books at their disposal, and in the 1830s it was his library, and his readiness to lend books, that saved him from complete social ostracism after his return to England. The unsolved mystery of Heber's character is how far he used his collecting as a calculated way of acquiring social prestige and furthering his political ambitions. What is clear is that in the early nineteenth century, book collecting was a social activity, and that if we take Heber as our example, book collectors do after all belong in circles of learning.

References

1. *Gentleman's Magazine*, April 1836, p.412.
2. Robert Chambers, *The Book of Days* (1866), pp.645-6.
3. Heber to Edward Copleston, 31 January 1811: Bodleian Library, MS Eng. lett. d.309, f.27.
4. A. N. L. Munby, *Essays and Papers* (1977), pp.225-34, based largely on the correspondence between Reginald and Richard Heber, Bodleian Library MS Eng. lett. c.204. From Munby's file on Heber (King's College, Cambridge, Munby papers box 1) it is clear that this was part of a larger project on Heber which remained unfinished at the time of his death; unfortunately, few of his notes survive.
5. *Morning Chronicle*, 23 December 1833. Arthur Freeman has suggested to me that the author of this memoir of Heber may have been Thomas Hill.
6. Elizabeth to Richard Heber, 15 March 1803: Bodleian Library, MS Eng. lett. c.207, f.40-1; Elizabeth to Richard Heber, 15 December 1802: *ibid.*, f.27.
7. R. H. Cholmondeley, *The Heber Letters 1783-1832* (1950).

8. Heber proposed Walter Scott for membership of the Club in 1822 (National Library of Scotland, MS 3895, f.272-3) and Francis Douce and Sir Thomas Phillipps were among the fellow-bibliophiles he proposed for membership of the Athenaeum (Bodleian Library MS Douce d.24, f.294, and MS Phillipps-Robinson b.115, f.190-2).

9. *Gentleman's Magazine*, January 1834, p.109.

10. Scott to John Leyden, 5 July 1806: *Letters*, vol.1 (1932), p.308.

11. Heber to Copleston, 31 January 1811: Bodleian Library, MS Eng. lett. d.309.

12. *Gentleman's Magazine*, April 1836, p.413.

13. Bodleian Library, MS Eng.misc. c.407, f.65-8.

14. Folger Shakespeare Library, Y.d.24 (Nichols papers), bundle 6, no.21: slightly abridged in the *Gentleman's Magazine*, April 1836, p.412.

15. Heber to Routh, 13 August 1811: Magdalen College, Oxford, MS 475 (iii) f.28.

16. Heber's bibliographical memoranda were, for the mot part, removed from the books and sold in one lot at the end of the Heber sale (*Bibliotheca Heberiana* XII.1689), but a few survive *in situ* (e.g. Folger Library, STC 19298) and record his instructions to the binder. His flyleaf notes frequently record the cost of the binding, and occasionally (e.g. Bodleian Library, 4° C 25 Art.BS and Auct. II. Q.5.58) the number of hours' work that the binding took.

17. Heber's copy of the Fazakerley sale catalogue is Bodleian Library Mus. Bibl. III. 8°. 329.

18. Heber to Scott, 2 April 1808: National Library of Scotland, MS 3877 (letters to Scott), ff.1-2.

19. Richard to Reginald Heber, 27 September 1808: Heber-Percy family papers, Hodnet Hall, Shropshire. I am grateful to Mr A. E. H. Heber-Percy for permission to consult these papers.

20. *Bibliotheca Heberiana* VI.3920.

21. *Bibliotheca Heberiana* IV.1835-7, IV.2475, VI.3217-8, VII.4568.

22. Folger Shakespeare Library, Y.d.24, bundle 6, no.21; slightly abridged in the *Gentleman's Magazine*, April 1836, p.412.

23. Heber's pocket diaries are Bodleian Library MSS Eng. misc. g.62-74.

24. Heber's coins and medals were sold by Stanley on 12-14 May, and his prints, drawings and paintings on 15-19 May 1834. As with the books, there is a concentration on Italian art to the relative neglect of Northern Europe, though Heber did own a small group of Durer engravings (lots 234-252 in the sale of prints). I am grateful to Giles Mandelbrote for drawing to my attention the data on Heber's art purchases held by the Getty Art History Information Program.

25. Dibdin to Spencer, 20 December 1816: British Library, Althorp MS G333.

26. Duke of Buckingham to Dibdin, 24 December 1817: Dibdin, *Reminiscences of a Literary Life* (1836), vol.2, p.611.

27. Dibdin to Spencer, 11 August 1815: British Library, Althorp MS G333.

28. John Carter, *Taste and Technique in Book-Collecting* (Cambridge, 1948), pp.14-15.

29. Drury to Dibdin, 15 September 1834: Bodleian Library, MS Eng. misc. d.85-6 (papers relating to Dibdin's *Reminiscences*), f.25.

30. Dibdin, *Reminiscences*, vol.2, p.940.

31. Alexander Dyce, *Reminiscences*, ed. Richard J. Schrader (Ohio, 1972), p.166.

32. Dibdin to Spencer, 2 December 1812: British Library, Althorp MS G332. Dibdin to Spencer, 17 November 1833: Northamptonshire Record Office, Spencer archives (temporary classmark SOX 106).
33. Heber to unknown correspondent, 11 March 1813: Cambridge University Library, Add MS 8202 (Munby autograph collection), no.41.
34. *Bibliotheca Heberiana*, IV.158. 'What was my astonishment on finding the *Tavistock Boecius . . .*' wrote Dibdin when he visited Pimlico after Heber's death (letter to Spencer, 17 November 1833, Northamptonshire Record Office SOX 106). There is no copy of the book in *Bibliotheca Spenceriana*, which may explain why Heber did not tell Dibdin that he owned a copy.
35. *Modern Midnight Conversation* was bought by Heber in 1806 ('Meyrick Sale at Kings') for 6s. 6d., sold as part of *Bibliotheca Heberiana*, IV.1506, and is now Bodleian Library Vet. A5. f.114.
36. Heber's famous dislike of large-paper copies (for which see *Gentleman's Magazine*, January 1834, p.109, and *Literary Gazette*, 23 November 1833, p.747) is corroborated by a letter to Routh: 'You were correct in supposing I should prefer the *small* Paper to the large.' (Magdalen College, Oxford, MS 475 (iii), f.62).
37. Carter, *Taste and Technique*, p.85.
38. *Morning Chronicle*, 23 December 1833.
39. Turner to C. H. Hartshorne, 27 May 1825: Northamptonshire Record Office, X7225 album B, no.109.
40. *Morning Chronicle*, Monday 2 December 1833.
41. A copy of the Lort catalogue in the Folger Shakespeare Library (shelfmark Z997 L85 Cage) identifies the private collectors who bid under fictitious names (Steevens was 'Froissart', Douce was 'Fabian' and so on). It is possible that this gave Dibdin the idea for the pseudonyms in his *Bibliomania*. According to the *Morning Chronicle* (23 December 1833) Heber's principal opponent among the booksellers was John Cuthell, who 'paid Heber in his own coin — by running up a book beyond its value, and then permitting Heber to be the purchaser — vehemently exclaiming, "Let the Oxford bookseller have it." '
42. Terry to Walter Scott, 30 June 1812: Wilfred Partington, ed., *The Private Letter-Books of Sir Walter Scott* (1930), pp.23-4.
43. Dibdin to Spencer, 8 July 1814: BL Althorp MS G332. Chalmers to David Laing, 19 February 1819: Edinburgh University Library, La.IV.6.
44. *Morning Chronicle*, 2 December 1833.
45. Heber to Phelps, 30 March 1816: Folger Shakespeare Library, Z997 G67 Cage.
46. Heber to Triphook, n.d.: Houghton Library, Harvard, bMS Eng. 1106.1.
47. Dibdin to Spencer (on the Bindley sale), 25 January 1819: BL Althorp MS G334.
48. *Morning Chronicle*, 2 December 1833. On rates of commission, see Munby, *Phillipps Studies*, vol.3, pp.49-50.
49. Thorpe to Heber, 4 April 1826: Bodleian Library, MS Eng. lett. c.208, f.25; Thorpe to Heber, n.d. (April-May 1826), *ibid.*, f.31.
50. Thorpe to Heber, postmarked 9 February 1827: Bodleian Library, MS Eng. misc. b.78, f.33.
51. Chalmers to David Laing, 29 September 1815: Edinburgh University Library, La.IV.6.

52. Thorpe to Heber, 23 October 1826: Bodleian Library, MS Eng. lett. c.208, f.60. William Stevenson Fitch to Dawson Turner, 29 December 1833: Trinity College, Cambridge, uncatalogued Turner correspondence.

53. Heber to Blackwood, 22 May 1812: National Library of Scotland, MS 4001 (Blackwood papers), f.95. There is a copy of Blackwood's *Catalogue of a valuable collection of books . . . for the year 1812* in the National Library of Scotland, shelfmark NG.1611.d.6.

54. Heber's copy of the Dampier sale catalogue is Bodleian Library Mus. Bibl. III. 8°. 308ª, and his copy of the Gordonstoun sale catalogue is Folger Shakespeare Library Z997 G67 Cage.

55. Park to Walter Scott, 23 June 1812: Wilfred Partington, ed., *Sir Walter's Post-Bag* (1932), p.89. Heber to Routh, 11 July 1812: Magdalen College, Oxford, MS 475 (iii), f.30. Sidney Lee, *Shakespeare's Comedies, Histories, & Tragedies . . . A Census of Extant Copies* (Oxford 1902), p.15.

56. Heber to Scott, 16 June 1812: National Library of Scotland, MS 3883 (letters to Scott), f.9.

57. As in the case of Caxton's edition of *The Pylgremage of the Sowle* (1483) (*Bibliotheca Heberiana*, IV.2686) for which Spencer offered Heber £262.10, and which Heber later bought back at Spencer's duplicate sale in March 1821 (bought by 'Lister', probably Heber bidding under a pseudonym): see Seymour de Ricci, *A Census of Caxtons* (1909), pp.78-9.

58. *Literary Gazette*, 23 November 1833, p.747.

59. *Gentleman's Magazine*, January 1834, p.107.

60. 'Of the Living Poets of Great Britain' (1810), in Kenneth Curry, ed., *Sir Walter Scott's Edinburgh Annual Register* (Knoxville, 1977).

61. Dibdin to Spencer, 1 September 1812: BL Althorp MS G332.

62. Heber to Scott, postmarked 31 March 1800: National Library of Scotland, MS 3874 (letters to Scott), ff.60-1.

63. Richard to Reginald Heber, 4 March 1809: Heber-Percy muniments, Hodnet Hall.

64. Richard to Reginald Heber, 10 June 1809: Hodnet Hall.

65. Folger Shakespeare Library, PR 1205 E38 Cage.

66. An undated letter from Heber, possibly to Thomas Park, asks his correspondent to 'give my servant . . . the copy of Vol II of the Specimens' (National Library of Scotland MS 962, f.107). This is the only direct evidence of his involvement in the publication of the book, but his obituary in the *Literary Gazette* (26 October 1833) states that he 'superintended the publication of the third edition', and an incomplete set of the fourth edition 'with several proof-sheets of the work, having MS Additions and Corrections in the Editor's [*i.e.* Heber's] handwriting, inserted' was lot 177 in J. P. Collier's sale, 7-9 August 1884 (I owe this reference to Janet Freeman).

67. Heber to Laing, 4 December 1820: Edinburgh University Library, La.IV.6.

68. Heber's letters to Routh are in Magdalen College, Oxford, MSS 464 and 475; Routh's letters to him are in the Bodleian Library, MS Eng. lett. d.209.

69. Frodsham Hodson to Heber, 6 November 1806: *The Heber Letters*, p.214.

70. Lord Spencer to H. B. Harrison, 14 July 1821: Magdalen College, Oxford, MS 475 (iii), f.55.

71. Magrath to Turner, 13 November 1833: Trinity College, Cambridge, O.14.11 (94). Dibdin to Spencer, 12 November 1833: Northamptonshire Record Office, Spencer

archives (temporary classmark SOX 106). I am grateful to Dr Paul Hopkins for drawing the Dibdin letters in the Northamptonshire Record office to my attention.

72. Dibdin to Spencer, 6 July 1821: BL Althorp MS G334. *Literary Gazette*, 23 November 1833, p.747.
73. Stanhope to Heber, 7 October 1824: Bodleian Library, MS Eng. lett. d.209, f.195.
74. Richard to Reginald Heber (*'Most private'*), 16 January 1823: Hodnet Hall. Reginald to Richard Heber: Bodleian Library, MS Eng. lett. d.202, f.185.
75. See my article 'A Study in Bibliomania: Charles Henry Hartshorne and Richard Heber', *Book Collector*, vol.42, no.1 (Spring 1993), pp.24-43, and no.2 (Summer 1993), pp.185-212.
76. G. S. Rousseau has investigated the links between antiquarianism and homosexuality in his essays 'The sorrows of Priapus' and 'Love and antiquities', reprinted in his *Perilous Enlightenment: pre- and post-modern discourses sexual, historical* (Manchester, 1991). For Knight's *Prolegomena*, see *Bibliotheca Heberiana*, VII.3359.
77. Munby, *Phillipps Studies*, vol.3, pp.73-4. Phillipps's copy of the sale catalogue, *Catalogue des livres, la plupart rares et précieux* (Paris, 1829), with his annotations, is in Cambridge University Library, Munby d.188.
78. Heber to Routh, 13 August 1811: Magdalen College, Oxford, MS 475 (iii), f.28.
79. Richardson to Heber, 17 February 1826: Bodleian Library, MS Eng. lett. d.210, f.89.
80. Richardson to Heber, 20 February 1828: Bodleian Library, MS Eng. lett. d.210, f.91; Richardson to Heber, 11 December 1829: *ibid.*, f.97. The mortgage deed is at Hodnet. Magrath claimed in 1833 that Heber's Yorkshire estates had also been mortgaged to 'a Lady, I presume Miss Currer'. I can find no evidence to support this, although a Currer family account book (sold at Bloomsbury Book Auctions, 6 April 1995, lot 212) records a series of loans to Heber, including one of £1000 in 1823, and a corresponding series of interest payments (usually overdue). If a match between Miss Currer and Heber was ever seriously considered, it probably had more to do with uniting their respective Yorkshire estates than combining their libraries.
81. Dyce to Collier, 21 August 1831: Folger Shakespeare Library, MS Y.d.341 (56). I owe this reference to Janet Freeman.
82. Mary Cholmondeley (*née* Heber) to Routh, 9 October 1833: Magdalen College, Oxford, MS 475 (iii), f.64; Magrath to Turner, 13 November 1833: Trinity College, Cambridge, O.14.11 (94).
83. Heber to Messrs Lackington & Co., 24 May 1820: BL Add MS 28653 (Upcott autograph collection), f.197.
84. Dibdin, *Reminiscences*, vol.1, pp.436-7. Thorpe wrote in 1826 that 'all I have bought hitherto . . . that is since you have been on the Continent' had been sent to Heber's London house: Bodleian Library, MS Eng. lett. c.208, f.66.
85. Dibdin to Spencer, 17 November 1833: Northamptonshire Record Office, Spencer archives (temporary classmark SOX 106).
86. Heber's will is dated 1 September 1827, and was proved on 13 January 1834; there is a copy in the Heber-Percy muniments at Hodnet Hall.
87. The twelve-part sale of the library in London realized £56,774; the two Paris sales made about 18,000 francs each; the drawings, prints and paintings fetched £1273. I hope to tell the story of the Heber sales in another article.
88. *Gentleman's Magazine*, January 1834, p.107.

The sale of the Luttrell Psalter

JANET BACKHOUSE

THE DIFFICULTY of attracting funds for the purchase of a major 'heritage' item offered on the open market, without at the same time exciting so much interest as to raise its price, is no new one. On 12 January 1929 the Director of the British Museum, Sir Frederick Kenyon, faced the depressing task of informing his Trustees that one of Britain's most celebrated medieval works of art, the Luttrell Psalter, which had been on loan to the Museum's Department of Manuscripts for some three decades, was on its way to the sale room. He had already taken steps to ascertain what could be done to ensure that the manuscript remained in England but the response he had received, notably from the National Art Collections Fund, was not encouraging, owing to a number of other commitments. To make matters worse, though this was not as yet laid before the Trustees, another manuscript of comparable stature and from the same private source, the early fifteenth-century Psalter and Hours made in England for John Duke of Bedford, seemed likely to share the same fate. This second book had been totally unknown to scholars before its deposit at the Museum only a few weeks earlier and a description of it was being prepared for publication in the New Palaeographical Society's series by excited members of the Museum's own staff.

A brief and cautious outline of the cliffhanging saga which ensued was published three years later by Eric Millar in the introduction to his comprehensive edition of the Luttrell Psalter.[1] However, it has since emerged that he personally retained until his death in 1966 a file of sensitive correspondence and notes recording his view of the transaction and shedding fresh light on what went on behind the scenes during the next few months. This file was transferred to the British Museum along with his generous bequest of manuscripts, drawings and watercolours but, falling into no special category, was shelved with odd notes and miscellanea relating to his private collection. Read in conjunction with material in the archives of the Department of Manuscripts and in the central archives of the British Museum, it presents a very lively record of one of the most important acquisitions of the present century.[2] Almost 70 years have passed since these events took place. All the chief protagonists are now dead and cannot therefore be embarrassed by them. Readers should remember that at the time in question most of the 'heritage' safety net which today provides at least a stay of execution was far in the future. There were no provisions for acceptance in lieu of inheritance taxes, no tax advantages on private treaty sales to public collections, no reviewing committee appeals to offer a possibly vital delay of export and no National Heritage Memorial Funds. Only the National Art Collections Fund, set up by private subscription in 1903, was likely to offer any kind of immediate assistance in these circumstances.

The Luttrell Psalter, written and illuminated early in the fourteenth century for Sir Geoffrey Luttrell of Irnham in Lincolnshire, is one of the world's most famous medieval works of art. The lively and colourful scenes of everyday life that enliven its Latin pages have been reproduced in countless popular history books over the last two centuries (fig.1). The manuscript first came to public attention in 1794, when the miniature of Sir Geoffrey with his wife and daughter-in-law was reproduced for Richard Gough the antiquary.[3] It was then already in the hands of the staunchly Catholic Weld family, owners of Lulworth Castle in Dorset where they had lived since the time of the Civil War. In 1672 William Weld of Lulworth had married Elizabeth Sherborne, sister of Nicolas Sherborne of Stonyhurst, through whom the manuscript descended. In 1839 a generous selection of subjects from the Psalter was engraved for *Vetusta Monumenta*[4] and the book thereafter came to be regarded as a prime source of information on the activities and pastimes of its period. Towards the end of 1896 the Trustees of the Lulworth Settled Estates decided to deposit it in the British Museum, where it could be made available for study and display. In the following year the Trustees of the Museum were asked for a formal receipt, specifying the conditions under which it would be kept. The relevant minute records: 'The application is made on the suggestion of the Master in Lunacy.' The manuscript was removed in June 1906 but redeposited in December 1909, and remained peacefully in the Department of Manuscripts until the late summer of 1928.[5]

During this time the Lulworth estates were tenanted by two long-lived bachelor brothers. Reginald Joseph Weld, who succeeded in 1877, died at the age of 81 in August 1923. He was followed by 69-year-old

Fig.1.   The Luttrell Psalter. Depiction of harrowing. The Luttrell arms are displayed in the right-hand margin. BL Add. MS 42,130, f.171. *Reproduced by permission of The British Library Board.*

Humphrey Joseph Weld, an intervening brother, Shireburn Joseph Weld, having died, also unmarried, in 1915.[6] On 18 August 1928 the Director of the British Museum received a first intimation of coming trouble in the form of a letter from the Lulworth Trustees suggesting that the manuscript ought to be insured at the expense of the Museum. The question of replacing or repairing the book's seventeenth-century binding was also raised, this expense too being regarded as the responsibility of the Museum. The wear and tear of more than two centuries was claimed to be entirely due to handling and display during the Psalter's sojourn in Bloomsbury. It was explained that the Treasury would make no provision for insurance premiums in respect of manuscripts on loan to the national collection. However, Hugh Smith of the National Art Collections fund did feel that it might be possible to find money for the binding. This was already under discussion when, on 26 August, Humphrey Weld died and the Lulworth estate passed to his first cousin, Herbert Joseph Weld. The British Museum authorities already quite clearly felt extremely disquieted about the future of the Psalter. In a note dated 29 August, Sir Frederick Kenyon wrote to the Keeper of Manuscripts, Julius Parnell Gilson, that Hugh Smith would hardly care to rebind the book 'for the benefit of a new owner or American purchaser'.

Born on 7 January 1852, the new owner of Lulworth was already widely known as a traveller and explorer in Africa and Arabia, as the initiator of excavations in Iraq which had resulted in a large collection of artefacts being given to the Ashmolean Museum in Oxford, and as a hunter and naturalist, having collected substantial numbers of specimens for the natural History Museum.[7] Originally named Herbert Weld Blundell, his father having adopted the additional surname on inheriting the Ince Blundell estates in Lancashire, together with their famous collections of art and antiquities, he reverted to the single name of Weld by deed poll in 1924, presumably in anticipation of his inheritance of Lulworth. In 1923 he had married Theodora Morrison whose father, David McLaren Morrison, was the author of several elegantly presented little books of Victorian moral philosophy including (1895) *Life's Prescription in Seven Doses*. She was to die on 23 December 1928, only weeks after her husband came into the estate, after which all his letters are written on traditionally black-bordered notepaper.

Herbert Weld first addressed himself directly to the Museum on 11 September, asking if someone could be recommended to examine old documents and letters at Lulworth. At the same time he stressed that he had no desire to withdraw the Luttrell Psalter from the Museum's care and enquired about the possibility of commissioning some reproductions from it. Gilson himself replied with a lengthy and helpful letter and was dismayed when Weld wrote again, on 29 September, having now seen the earlier exchanges with the representatives of the family Trust, stating: 'I am afraid I cannot give any assurance that the book will remain in the British Museum, simply because in these days no-one can say he owns anything in the face of Death duties that are expressly devised to break up & confiscate settled estates. I am afraid it is probable that it will have to be sold – but if not I shall be glad to let it remain in the hands of the Museum.' However, at the end of October he brought to London two further illuminated books found at Lulworth, one of which turned out to be the magnificent Bedford Psalter and Hours, until then utterly unknown. A few days later he sent Mr Maggs to the Museum to see all three books and presumably to advise as to their value. On 17 November he wrote again to Gilson, who seems in the meantime to have raised the question of a possible direct sale of both major manuscripts to the Museum, in these terms: '. . . being heirlooms, they would be, I fancy, subject to the Courts' decision respecting their sale & I am afraid this would mean they would have to be sold by auction. In the light of the late sales of £30,000 for a MS of Alice in Wonderland & £4,000 for one of 13 copies of a modern printed book of the Kelmscott Press, it would be very hard I should think to fix a price that would satisfy the legal authorities that have to give permission for heirlooms to be sold.'[8]

The anticipated blow fell at the beginning of the New Year. In a letter dated 7 January, Herbert Weld authorized Geoffrey Hobson of Sotheby's to remove all three of his manuscripts from the Museum 'for the purpose of cataloguing etc.' The Luttrell Psalter was taken away next day. It was by no means certain that the manuscript would not be offered privately elsewhere, in spite of Weld's letter to Gilson, and in the absence of export controls there was nothing to prevent its being taken out of the country without further ado. Gilson at once wrote to Weld for a clear statement of his intentions, appealing to him once again: '. . . to give the nation the option of purchase at such price as your valuers may suggest. The Loutrell [sic] Psalter is so valuable a record of English medieval life that we think we may fairly ask that a private sale should not be concluded without giving to the national collection an opportunity of purchase. It seems probable that the court might agree to sanction a sale at a price settled between your valuers and the Museum. I think there are precedents.' Weld responded on 11 January, with dramatic effect, that he would do his best to keep the manuscripts in England as: 'Nothing short of confiscation which death duties are often the equivalent of would make me part with them.'

Meanwhile, on the very day that had seen the removal of the Psalter from the Museum, Eric Millar dispatched a private letter to Belle da Costa Greene, a dear and valued friend and colleague, custodian of the Pierpont Morgan collection in New York. He had spent several happy weeks in the States during the previous summer, studying material at the Morgan Library, and had become very friendly with Miss Greene and well known to her employer, John Pierpont Morgan.[9] She seems already to have been fully apprised of the situation and he told her: '. . . we should be enormously grateful to Mr Morgan if he would resist any private offer of the books, and if you would help us by giving to Rosenbach and any others who may occur to you a hint to the same effect we should appreciate it more than I can say. You know the importance of the Loutrell Psalter as a national monument, and I am afraid that if it comes into public auction it will have all the added publicity resulting from its deposit here: it has been in constant use in the Students' Room, and it is almost as bad as if one of our best Museum books, such as Queen Mary's Psalter, were to come up for sale.'

Reaction from America was heartening. Pierpont Morgan himself contacted Kenyon, who had addressed him personally, and the generous scheme that was eventually to secure the purchase of both manuscripts began to take shape. Belle Greene wrote to Eric Millar, obviously giving rather more than a simple hint, to report that she had: '. . . seen the dealers, Rosenbach, and Lathrop Harper here, both of whom have agreed to "stay off" the Louterell [sic] Psalter. The auction people had already written to Rosenbach "inviting" his best interest for the sale! . . . Let me know, as soon as possible after receipt of this your idea of the highest price it might fetch, and cannot you find out from Sotheby if a reserve has been placed upon it?' At the beginning of February Pierpont Morgan made a firm offer to put up the money for the purchase of the Psalter and to hold it at the Museum's disposal for a year, thus providing a specific target for a public appeal. At the same time this would guarantee that, should the appeal fail, the manuscript would be in an appropriate and accessible home, albeit on the other side of the Atlantic, as it would automatically revert to Morgan.[10]

On 6 February 1929 the Bedford Psalter and Hours followed the Luttrell Psalter to Sotheby's. At the same time Gilson discussed with the auctioneers the order in which they anticipated putting up the two manuscripts. On behalf of Sotheby's Charles Des Graz acceded to his request that the Luttrell Psalter should be offered first, which would relieve the Museum of the need to jeopardize its chances of success by bidding first for what was regarded as the lesser item. In return he asked Gilson for an advance proof of the description of the Bedford manuscript prepared for the New Palaeographical Society, as an aid to his own cataloguing. This Gilson eventually conceded with great reluctance, with the justification that it might possibly be already in print by the time of the sale. Des Graz responded sharply: 'We felt sure that Mr Weld, after lending his property to the Museum for so long, could count on your help in getting the best price for it when he is compelled to sell.' Three weeks later Weld also applied to Gilson to send a copy of the piece to Sotheby's, hinting: 'I am in hopes that, if one fetches sufficient, to be able to withdraw the other and leave it in the B.M.'

As soon as Pierpont Morgan became aware of the existence of the Bedford manuscript and learned that it too was to be put up for sale, he extended his original offer to cover both books. By the beginning of March his plans had been finalized and were fully set out in a letter to Kenyon dated 7 March.[11] He had decided in his own mind: '. . . that we are not being unfair to anyone else, even in asking them to stand aside. . . . As far as I am concerned, therefore, if you would instruct Quaritch to buy both manuscripts, I should recommend that you do not put any limit on them, as any limit decided upon might be just a bit too low.' The loan, however large, was to be interest free. He added, as an important safeguard, that he was to be regarded as acting for the Pierpont Morgan Library as its President and not in any private capacity: '. . . therefore the contract into which I have entered with the British Museum, as set forth in the letters that have passed between us, does not depend in any way upon my personal existence.' Belle Greene felt some misgivings about her employer's decision and expressed them in a personal letter to Millar on 2 April. Although she was '. . . absolutely in accordance with him in his original offer to make the acquisition of the Louterell Psalter certain by underwriting it', she felt that to extend the scheme to embrace the Bedford book as well was possibly unwise.

It could place an intolerably large burden upon the Museum and, should the second manuscript eventually pass to Morgan, it might give rise to criticism. However: '. . . he is always right in his judgements, so I daresay all will turn out well.' Strictest secrecy was of course enjoined all round.

According to Millar's official published account of events, anxiety was now effectively removed. The manuscripts, if lost to the nation, '. . . would go to the best possible home abroad.' The sale had been fixed for 29 July and it only remained to wait. The ensuing four months were not however to pass without incident. In May Gilson, now in his 61st year, was taken ill. On 23 May he underwent an operation for appendicitis. On 16 June he died, after eighteen years as Keeper of Manuscripts and Egerton Librarian, and Harold Idris Bell replaced him as head of department. As a result of this unexpected loss the final stages of the drama bore more heavily upon Eric Millar personally than he could originally have anticipated. The secrecy surrounding the transaction with Morgan inevitably had its drawbacks. On 2 July the managing director of Quaritch, F. S. Ferguson, directed a long letter to Belle Greene, revealing that he had received details of Morgan's involvement with the Luttrell bid from Gilson and from his successor and that it was rumoured that a final figure of £50,000 or more was expected. Gilson himself had regarded Ferguson's own estimate of £25-30,000 as unrealistically low. Offering to reduce his usual commission to a nominal 1%, Ferguson told Miss Greene that he anticipated receiving Morgan's direct instructions to buy the manuscript and furthermore indicated that he expected him to enter a bid for the Bedford book on his own behalf. Morgan was greatly disturbed both by the fact that Ferguson knew of his offer to the Museum and by his ignorance of its extension to cover the Bedford Psalter and Hours. He cabled that he had expected the Museum to do its own buying, merely applying to him for the necessary funds, and a mollifying response from Millar, in Kenyon's absence abroad, was telegraphed across the Atlantic on 17 July.

Meanwhile on 10 July Millar had received a phone call from Francis Needham at the Bodleian Library, suggesting that his institution should make an effort to secure the Bedford manuscript. Millar attempted tactfully to dissuade him without letting any cats out of their bags, following up the conversation with a letter approved by both Kenyon and Bell. Two days later Needham called at the Museum and told Millar that, even after a meeting with Kenyon and Arundell Esdaile, the

Museum's Secretary, he was still under the impression that the Museum was concentrating solely on the Luttrell Psalter. He himself was therefore attempting to interest a millionaire benefactor in the purchase of the second manuscript for the benefit of Oxford! Millar again did his best to put him off and extracted a promise that he would let the Museum know of any further developments. Millar then hastened round to the Director's Office with Bell: '. . . and found as I expected that statements that we would "consider the claims of a friendly rival" etc did not come from K[enyon], & were evidently supplied by Esdaile, who did not know of the arrangement for the Bedford Hours until I told him on the way out.' The next day, Saturday 13 July, Millar met Ferguson and discovered 'from a chance remark' that he had indeed not received instructions to bid for the Bedford book as well as the Luttrell. He had already given to an unnamed American customer an estimate of £12-15,000 on it and had also begun to interest Calouste Gulbenkian. Millar and Bell at once joined forces to put the matter straight with him.

On 17 July, the day of his cable to Morgan, Millar met Sir Alfred Chester Beatty, who had had a letter from Gulbenkian: '. . . objecting to the proposal that he should keep off the Bedford Horae.' Millar, urged by Beatty, advised Bell to contact Kenyon, then in Geneva, and seek approval to trust Gulbenkian with the facts. This was given and the task entrusted to Beatty himself, who seems already to have been fully informed, with the proviso that Morgan was to be described merely as 'an anonymous benefactor'. On 25 July Needham wrote to Millar giving a firm assurance that no bid would be placed on behalf of the Bodleian: '. . . so you may sleep easy o'nights, and dream that the Museum – or C(hester) B(eatty)? Aha! – has bought both the books for a song – as indeed I hope may happen.' This implies that Gulbenkian was to have been Oxford's benefactor and that he had taken Beatty's guarded disclosure as indicating that he was himself the Museum's good fairy.

By this time, only days before the date fixed for the sale, the press was beginning to take an interest in events. One of Millar's colleagues, Robin Flower, noted on 19 July that he had received a lady from the *Daily Chronicle* who had 'somewhat fanciful and exaggerated ideas' about the Luttrell Psalter. However, she did ask whether there was any truth in 'the rumour which had reached them of Americans standing down in favour of the British Museum'. Flower responded that: '. . . occasions had occurred in the past on which Americans had refrained from bidding when they felt an object would find its appropriate home in the Museum, but I could not say how far this was likely in the present case.' He must have been relieved that the matter was not aired in the resulting column.

While all this was going on, a much more complicated development was unfolding in the courts, totally unknown to the Museum authorities. Herbert Weld had been correct in assuming that legal sanction would be required before heirlooms governed by a family trust could be dispersed. He had not foreseen that a quirk of the current English law of inheritance would bar him from possessing them. It transpired that, under the terms of the resettlement of the Lulworth Settled Estates drawn up in September 1869, although he had quite legitimately inherited Lulworth itself in succession to his deceased cousin, the heirlooms and other chattels had, on the death of that cousin, become vested in the estate of the first of the tenants in tail to achieve his majority. A professional explanation of this somewhat complicated situation is printed in Millar's study of the Luttrell Psalter.[12] The heir in question was Richard Shireburn Weld Blundell, elder son of Herbert Weld's brother Charles, who had reached the age of twenty-one before being killed in action on 1 January 1916. It was adjudged in the High Court that the Weld heirlooms were now vested absolutely in the estate of his widow and personal representative. This judgement was upheld in the Court of Appeal.

Richard Weld Blundell's widow, born Angela Mary Mayne, was by coincidence herself a cousin of the family, being a granddaughter of Sir Frederick Aloysius Weld of Chideock, one-time Governor of Western Australia. In 1927 she had remarried and was now the wife of Alfred Noyes the poet, author of 'Come down to Kew in lilac time'. According to the account given in her new husband's memoirs,[13] Herbert Weld had contacted her some months earlier, revealing that the terms of the family settlement might give her an interest in the Luttrell Psalter and suggesting that, as he was planning to sell it to meet death duties on the estate (no small matter after two deaths in five years), they might come to some agreement over the proceeds. Application had been made to a judge in chambers for permission to sell. Mrs Noyes is reported by her husband to have replied that she was happy to make no claim to the book and that, as far as she was concerned, he was quite at liberty to dispose of it.

The change of ownership was reported just three days before the day of the auction. Again according to the memoirs of Alfred Noyes,

Kenyon at once called round at his house in Hanover Terrace, Regents Park, to attempt to persuade Mrs Noyes to withdraw the manuscripts from Sotheby's and offer them direct to the British Museum at an agreed valuation. At the same time a director of Sotheby's, anticipating Kenyon's strategy, arrived at the house and begged Alfred Noyes to influence his wife to leave them in the saleroom. Mrs Noyes, reportedly anxious to see the books safely in the national collection, promised Kenyon that she would let him know later in the day at what sum they could be withdrawn.

Two memoranda preserved by Eric Millar reveal that matters were not quite as straightforward and above board as the Noyes account implies. The first is in the hand of Harold Idris Bell and reports a conversation with Kenyon at 2.30 p.m. on Friday, 26 July, presumably directly after his return from Hanover Terrace. It reads:

Owners prepared to deal direct if they can satisfy themselves as to question of death duties. Are consulting solicitors. If MSS. can be withdrawn will deal direct. If sale proceeds they wd. prefer MSS. to be bought in, as by arrangement they will not then have to pay commission. They are therefore thinking of high reserve price, wh. they will communicate before sale. Ferguson to be instructed in that case not to carry bidding up to reserve price, *but if when this is reached any outsider comes in he is to resume bidding.* Price wh. will be considered for L.P. is £25,000; for B.H. reserve price is £15,000 (under consideration); K. suggested 8000-10000. Thinks we cd. get both for £35,000 or might go up to £40,000 if necessary.

Clear-headed Millar was obviously horrified by the implications of this dubious scheme, and seems to have feared that Kenyon and Bell were in some danger of agreeing to it. Later on the same day he typed a long letter to Bell, setting out all the possibilities. As he saw it, two courses were available. The owners of the manuscripts could, preferably, offer them to the Museum at an agreed price. In this case the Museum could perhaps make the gesture of offering to pay all or part of Sotheby's lost commission in order to avoid public sale. On the other hand the course outlined by Bell could be adopted. Of this he wrote:

This course seems to me to be open to at least two grave objections.

(1) We stand pledged to Mr Morgan to buy both MSS. at any cost, with his money. An unlimited commission has been given by us for this purpose to Quaritch, Mr Morgan's avowed object being to save the MSS. if possible for the British Museum, but otherwise to secure them absolutely and beyond all doubt for the Morgan Library. He has left all the arrangements, which he would

otherwise have made himself, in our hands, undertaking to hold the MSS. for a year, not only charging no interest on the money but promising to contribute £500 towards the cost in the event of our being able to make the purchase.

If as a result of the sale the MSS. are not Mr Morgan's property at any figure and above all at a low one, he will be justified in thinking that we have not carried out our undertaking, and from my personal knowledge of Mr Morgan and of Miss Greene I feel certain that they will both adopt this attitude. The risk seems to me too great a one to contemplate from any point of view.

(2) The object of the proposed arrangement is admittedly to assist the vendors in avoiding Messrs. Sotheby's commission, Messrs. Sotheby having apparently undertaken to waive the latter if the MSS. are bought in and remain the property of the vendors. If they are at once offered privately to us, will it not be open to Messrs. Sotheby to say that we have entered into a 'conspiracy' with the vendors? They will certainly demand their commission, while there is a risk that our future relations with Messrs. Sotheby and perhaps with the various collectors and dealers who have stood down in our favour will be seriously compromised.

(3) Is there not a great risk involved in the event of Quaritch retiring from the bidding and being forced to enter it again? This might well be taken as a sign that the Museum has bid its utmost and that Quaritch was now bidding for another client (e.g. Morgan) and the price might be forced up to almost any figure.

He concluded that the only safe strategy was to stand by the plan already made as: 'We have little to gain and may lose everything by any other course.'

Whether his advice was heeded or whether the authorities themselves thought better of it, the scheme to circumvent Sotheby's commission was abandoned. Mrs Noyes agreed to sell the Luttrell Psalter direct to the British Museum for 30,000 guineas (£31,500), effectively committing the Museum's Trustees to its eventual acquisition. The Bedford Psalter and Hours was duly offered in the saleroom on 29 July with a reserve of £30,000 and was knocked down to Quaritch for £33,000, after which a prepared statement was read, revealing that it had been bought by an anonymous benefactor for the benefit of the British Museum. The identity of the benefactor came out in *The Times* on 5 August, with Morgan's consent.[14] 'Both MSS. secured for joint total £64,000. White hot greetings and gratitude,' ran Millar's ecstatic cable to Belle Greene. 'Thousand thanks your cable especially the new kind of love,' responded Miss Greene.

On the afternoon of the day of the sale Bell and Millar attended a meeting of National Art Collections Fund representatives, at which it was agreed that the Fund should negotiate a contribution to be matched by the Treasury which, together with £15,000 from the Museum's own purchase funds and sums already promised by members of the public, would effectively cover the price of the Luttrell Psalter. The Bedford Psalter and Hours could then become the focus of a separate appeal, though it would clearly be psychologically advantageous to continue to link the two books together until the appeal was completed. This arrangement was ratified at a meeting of a Museum Trustees' committee on 12 October. A special Treasury grant of £7,500 had by then been obtained, after correspondence between Kenyon and the Prime Minister. A certain amount of money was collected during the ensuing winter, but as late as May in the following year well over £20,000 was still required. In a letter to *The Times* on 26 May 1930 the Trustees appealed to 'the patriotic liberality of private benefactors' to save the day. In the event, with further very generous assistance from the NACF, the money was eventually raised, Morgan's loan repaid, and the two manuscripts were incorporated into the manuscript collections under the numbers Additional MS 42130 (the Luttrell Psalter) and Additional MS 42131 (the Bedford Psalter and Hours). Public contributions finally totalled £18,107. 13s. 6d. and ranged from Mr Dyson Perrins' generous £1,000 to an anonymous shilling. A full list of the several hundred benefactors was published in Millar's volume on the Luttrell Psalter.[15]

Although the manuscripts had passed out of the hands of both parties, the sale itself did not mark the end of the story for either Herbert Weld or Mary Noyes. Exactly a month later the Weld family seat, Lulworth Castle in Dorset, was mysteriously burned to the ground overnight. Only prompt action by an army unit providentially stationed nearby saved the contents – including the heirlooms now enjoyed by Mrs Noyes – from destruction. The Noyes family, staying at the time with their Weld Blundell cousins in Lancashire, learned of the disaster from a dramatic photograph in *The Times*.[16] Two substantial sales soon followed. On 20 February 1930 Christie's sale of old English furniture included 99 lots consigned by Mrs Noyes, and on 3 March printed books and manuscripts selected from the library at Lulworth were offered by Sotheby's. Both catalogues describe the items as: 'Removed in consequence of the Fire.' Herbert Weld's understandable feelings of grievance were expressed in print, first in the correspondence columns of *Country Life* and later in *The Times*, shortly after the Museum had announced the successful conclusion of negotiations for the two great manuscripts.[17] In his eagerness to attack both the law of inheritance and the current estate duty arrangements he contrived to present a somewhat confused account of the situation, to which Major Rudolph Mayne and Messrs Lee, Bolton and Lee successively responded on behalf of Mrs Noyes.

However, in 1931 she found herself embroiled in further, and potentially serious, legal proceedings when she was sued by Mrs Lilian Westby, widow, of Morpeth Terrace, for payment of commission of £832. 10s. for her services in bidding up the Bedford Psalter and Hours two years earlier. The case was very fully reported in the press,[18] and was vigorously defended by Mrs Noyes. Her solicitors briefed Walter Monckton, KC (so soon afterwards to gain a place in another sphere of history for his involvement in the Abdication crisis in 1936) to appear on her behalf. According to Mrs Westby, she had been asked by Mrs Noyes, over a cup of tea on 25 July 1929, to bid for both manuscripts in the saleroom on the following Monday. This was on the day before Sir Frederick Kenyon's initial meeting with Mrs Noyes at Hanover Terrace. Mrs Westby had lived for some time in the United States, where she had picked up an American accent, and it was thought that her participation in the bidding would imply a transatlantic interest in the sale, encouraging other bidders to compete. She had been instructed to keep well below the reserve price fixed, but in the event—and in spite of being ordered by Alfred Noyes on the morning of the sale not to bid at all— she was carried away by her enthusiasm and went up to £32,000, ending as the unidentified underbidder to Quaritch. Alfred Noyes insisted that she had indeed been told not to bid and it transpired that he himself had arranged for his wife's brother-in-law, Mr Gordon Daniels, to put the bidding up to £26,000. The jury found in favour of Mrs Noyes, accepting that Mrs Westby had not been offered a specific reward. However, Charles Des Graz, appearing on behalf of Sotheby's to give evidence on the matter of the reserve price agreed on, characterized the suggested course of events as: '. . . a most improper procedure and a direct contravention of the conditions of sale'. In view of the arrangement proposed to the representatives of the British Museum during those same few days before the sale, one cannot help but feel that Mrs Noyes's professed lack of interest in the worth of the Lulworth heirlooms does not stand up to scrutiny.

Meanwhile at the British Museum the two great manuscripts at the centre of all the excitements had been formally assimilated into their new surroundings. A major study of the Luttrell Psalter was immediately put in hand and appeared in 1932. Similar publication for the Bedford manuscript was not however undertaken and it was to be three decades before it became the subject of a special study over and above its detailed catalogue description.[19] Both manuscripts were duly rebound and each now bears, in letters of gold inside its front cover, the statement that it was: '. . . saved for the British nation by the generosity of an American citizen, John Pierpont Morgan'. His own collection, so rich in medieval masterpieces, is forever the poorer as a result of this unparalleled gesture of friendship to the British Museum.

Without Morgan's assistance the British Museum would certainly have had difficulty in aspiring to the purchase of both manuscripts. Their combined cost, even at the most optimistic estimate, would have been far beyond the reach of the normal purchase budget. The prices eventually arrived at, while well within the most pessimistic of the forecasts, were extremely high for the period. The highest sum realized in the Yates Thompson sales a decade earlier was £11,800 for the Hours of Jeanne de Navarre.[20] The Chester Beatty sales in 1932-3 achieved nothing even remotely comparable.[21] Neither price can however be regarded as a completely genuine barometer of the market. The Luttrell Psalter changed hands at an agreed valuation. The Bedford Psalter and Hours, although it changed hands at public auction, was the subject of so much backstage diplomacy on the part of the purchaser, countered by such blatant manipulation on the part of the vendor, that its price, eventually higher than that of the Luttrell Psalter, is far from reliable. It was however a benchmark for the sale of an illuminated manuscript, and particularly for an illuminated manuscript of English origin. Although effortlessly upstaged only some four years later by the £100,000 at which the Codex Sinaiticus was purchased for the Museum from the Russian government, by private agreement but largely by enthusiastic public subscription, the intervention of the Depression, followed by World War II, ensured that it remained a saleroom benchmark for a long time. Not until the Dyson Perrins Apocalypse achieved an auction price of £65,000 in 1959 did any single manuscript make a comparable leap upwards.[22]

References

1. E. G. Millar, *The Luttrell Psalter*, 1932, pp.7-8.
2. All the information on which this paper is based is drawn either from Millar's confidential file or from the Trustees' Minutes, unless otherwise indicated. I am very grateful to the British Museum archivist, Janet Wallace, for her help in locating references. Millar's file has now been returned to the archives of the Department of Manuscripts.
3. See John Carter, *Ancient Sculpture and Painting*, ii, pp.59-60 etc.
4. Vol.vi, pp.1-10, pls.xx-xxv.
5. The reason for this break in the loan is apparently not recorded.
6. A convenient pedigree is given in Millar, *op. cit.*, p.8.
7. *Who Was Who 1929-1940*, 1941, pp.1433-4.
8. The autograph manuscript of 'Alice's Adventures Underground' was sold at Sotheby's on 3 April 1928, lot 319, for £15,400 to Rosenbach. It is now Additional MS 46700 in the British Library and a full account of its history is given in the appropriate volume of the *Catalogue of Additions* (1979). On 18 April 1928, also at Sotheby's, one of the vellum copies of the Kelmscott Chaucer was knocked down to Quaritch for £4,000.
9. This is clear from letters addressed to him at the time by his uncle 'F. Anstey', author of *Vice Versa*, Additional MS 54261, ff.134-48.
10. Morgan's original letter to Kenyon, dated 1 February 1929, is in the British Museum archives. A second letter, dated 14 February, refines the scheme.
11. British Museum archives.
12. *Op. cit.*, pp.7-8.
13. Alfred Noyes, *Two Worlds for Memory*, 1953, chapter 36.
14. Messrs Lee, Bolton and Lee, solicitors to Mrs Noyes, wrote to Bell on 26 February 1931 to ask whether Morgan's interest had become public as early as 20 August 1929. A note by Bell at the top of this letter, now in Millar's file, records that consent for the disclosure was given in a letter on 31 July, just two days after the sale.
15. *Op. cit.*, on two unnumbered leaves bound at the end of the book. A very substantial collection of correspondence and papers relating to the appeal is preserved in the British Museum archives.
16. 30 August 1929. The fire excited correspondence on 3 September and plans for rebuilding were reported on 19 September.
17. *Country Life*, 1 and 15 March 1930; *The Times*, 30 July and 6 August 1930.
18. Millar collected extensive cuttings from *The Times*, 17, 18 and 24 July 1931 and from *The Glasgow Herald*, 24 July 1931.
19. See D. H. Turner, 'The Bedford Hours and Psalter', *Apollo*, lxxvi (1962), pp.109-30. The article was written to coincide with the 8th Council of Europe exhibition, "Europäische Kunst um 1400", held in Vienna in the summer of 1962.
20. Sotheby's sale catalogue, 3 June 1919, lot 5.
21. Sotheby's sale catalogues, 7 June 1932 and 9 May 1933.
22. Sotheby's sale catalogue, 1 December 1959, lot 58.

The illuminated manuscript collection
of Edmond de Rothschild

CHRISTOPHER DE HAMEL

I BELIEVE THAT the illuminated manuscript collection of Baron Edmond de Rothschild (1845-1934) was very possibly the greatest ever assembled by one man. Having said that, I rather regret having chosen him for this paper, for I fear that he may emerge as an anti-hero in the context of a symposium on circles of learning, and that I shall certainly have a difficult time defending the antiquarianism of my champion. Of the quality of his manuscripts, however, I am in no doubt.

Baron Edmond de Rothschild lived and assembled his library in Paris. He was of course a member of the great banking family, and one of the richest men in the western world. He was a passionate and articulate Zionist and a massive benefactor of the early Jewish settlements of Erez-Israel. Edmond de Rothschild is not at all famous as a collector of medieval manuscripts. Entries in biographical dictionaries mention that he maintained the Rothschild tradition for art collecting, but illuminated manuscripts do not figure especially among his published interests. Manuscripts from Baron Edmond's library have no ownership inscriptions or bookplates, were never catalogued (as far as I know) and, at least after about 1900, were not shown to other collectors or lent for exhibitions. After the collector's death the manuscripts were divided up among his heirs, and many were subsequently looted by the Nazis and were lost. Most of this paper then consists of an attempt to reconstruct what illuminated manuscripts were actually in the most enigmatic of modern manuscript collections.

I first began to wonder about Baron Edmond in 1977 when I was asked to write a review of the opulent catalogue of the illuminated manuscripts in the Rothschild Collection at Waddesdon Manor in Buckinghamshire.[1] The catalogue describes at length 26 medieval manuscripts of varying quality from the really extremely good to the relatively ordinary, including a number of fragments and several quite unexceptional provincial French Books of Hours. If this is our first glimpse of the Rothschild manuscript library, it is a rather disappointing one. Overall, as Professor J. J. G. Alexander wrote in his own review called 'Run-of-the-mill medieval' in the *Times Literary Supplement*,[2] the Rothschild manuscripts at Waddesdon are 'not. . . of great significance for their texts or palaeography . . . and a number of the manuscripts [are] of standard or even mediocre quality', assembled without especial discrimination and comparing unfavourably in importance with the collections of C. W. Dyson Perrins or Major J. R. Abbey. This does not sound promising. In his short preface to the catalogue, Professor Anthony Blunt explained that the manuscripts at Waddesdon came from the collection of Baron Edmond de Rothschild and were inherited by his elder son James Armand de Rothschild (1878-1957), who lived in England and who bequeathed Waddesdon Manor and much of its contents to the National Trust on his death. His widow subsequently offered fourteen manuscripts in lieu of death duties and presented twelve others to join the collections at Waddesdon.

The finest book which James had inherited from his father is still in private hands. It was published by Rosy Schilling in the *Burlington Magazine* in 1942, 'A Book of Hours from the Limbourg Atelier', beginning, 'When Durrieu in 1904 published his study on the *Très Riches Heures du Duc de Berry* at Chantilly, he referred to a Book of Hours of Baron Edmond de Rothschild, as being of the utmost interest. . . Since then no further particulars of this manuscript have appeared. Now it has been presented by Mr James A. de Rothschild for the Red Cross Sale in October at Messrs. Sotheby's'.[3] The Book of Hours was lot 112 in that desperate sale for charity during the London Blitz, 13 October 1942. Rosy Schilling attended the auction with Miss Margaret Mackenzie, who kindly sent me in 1992 a long account of the sale. Bidding began at £1000 and rose bid by bid to Maggs at £5800, a huge sum on those dark times and by far the most expensive item in the sale. 'Who has bought it ?', Miss Mackenzie asked her companion at tea afterwards; 'She smiled happily, "It is an Austrian, married to an American millionaire's daughter. . . The Austrian, now in the Army, told his agent to bid for any illuminated manuscript – I find this very satisfying. . ."', said Rosy Schilling. The fortunate buyer was, in fact, Count Antoine Seilern (1901-1978), and the book is now better known as the Seilern Hours.[4] It is the nearest thing to the style of the *Très Riches Heures* of the Duc de Berry as still remains outside a national collection. It was not part of the Seilern Bequest to the Courtauld, has apparently never been fully photographed, and remains one of the least known of very major illuminated manuscripts.

Discretion about ownership and access is very much in the Rothschild tradition. In 1936, the American art historian, the late Professor Millard Meiss, saw part of Edmond de Rothschild's manuscript collection in Paris, having arranged this through his Jewish family connections rather than through his international reputation as a scholar. Even he was refused permission to take notes and was not permitted to photograph any.[5] After the War, when the collection had been looted by the Nazis in Paris, the family are said to have written to Professor Meiss explaining that no one else had seen the collection and asking him for any photographs that might help recover the manuscripts actually stolen. Professor Meiss, of course, had to reply that he had been unable even to make notes. The moral (as Jonathan Alexander tells the story — and I owe it to him) is that every private collection should be documented, if only for the protection of the owner.

Large numbers of illuminated manuscripts and other books from the Rothschild library in Paris disappeared into the hands of the Nazis probably between September 1940 and April 1943. There are terrible tales and already half-legends and half-truths of vast processions of looted works of art being moved back to Germany during the occupation of France. For obvious reasons, this is a period extremely difficult to document in any detail. I owe one tantalizing story to Dr Anthony Hobson. In 1951 an important extra-illustrated copy of the Duc d'Aumont's sale catalogue of 1782 was brought into Sotheby's by a Mr Stig Wilton of Stockholm. It was catalogued as a designated property and it sold for £520.[6] It subsequently transpired that a French bookseller recalled selling the same book to Baron Edmond de Rothschild, and Mr Stig Wilton then recounted that he had at the end of the War been in the Red Cross, and one day in Warsaw in 1945 saw an abandoned railway truck filled with books and manuscripts in red morocco bindings. Wondering where these came from, and as the snow was falling (at least this is how the story is told), he reached up and took one book — the smallest — in the hope of discovering the origin of this extraordinary cargo. That railway truck in Warsaw (whatever it really was) could conceivably have contained a substantial portion of Baron Edmond's library.

Here we can bring in one major record. Maurice Ettinghausen was for a long time the Paris representative for Maggs, the London booksellers. In his autobiography, Ettinghausen recounted that he was called in by Baroness Adelaide de Rothschild, Edmond's widow, to make a list of manuscripts in her late husband's library in the Faubourg St-Honoré in June 1935.[7] Professor James Marrow, when working on the Waddesdon catalogue in the early 1970s, was shown by the late Mrs de Rothschild a copy of this list, in English, and he kindly gave me a photocopy of his transcription of it.[8] It records 102 items, with some gaps. It gives little actual information but has extremely concise title — Hours, Bible, Missal, etc. — with a number. Ettinghausen then wrote these same numbers in faint pencil on the top left inside corner of the upper cover of the manuscripts he was listing. This, then, is the list which H. P. Kraus refers to in his own autobiography in a story of how he sat in the reading room of the Pierpont Morgan Library one day puzzling over several manuscripts which had no ownership marks beyond numbers in pencil, when a reader at the adjacent table, subsequently revealed as James Marrow, rose up like a spectre and said 'Gentlemen, I think I can save you some trouble . . .' and he produced his list.[9] By matching the pencil numbers in extant manuscripts with those in the Ettinghausen list, we can often identify former Rothschild manuscripts. By means of this list, one can identify, for example, MSS 10 and 11 as volumes in relatively recent catalogues of Pierre Berès and H. P. Kraus respectively,[10] MSS 13 and 32 as manuscripts in Sotheby's sales in London in 1984 and 1991,[11] and MS 44 as a Dutch Book of Hours of c.1451 now in private hands in the Netherlands.[12]

Another important and little-known source for former Rothschild books is a thick, oblong, crudely-printed handlist prepared by the French military command in Germany in 1948, the *Répertoire des Biens Spoliés*, listing works of art reported as stolen from France during the War.[13] This is an extraordinary and heart-rending document mostly in French with parts in Russian, English and German, recording page after page of whole libraries which disappeared, with the names in the right-hand columns of those whose collections had been looted. The detail given depends entirely on the information supplied by those who reported losses. The Wildensteins, for example, who lost a great deal, had clearly kept meticulous records of their possessions. The names of three Rothschilds occur over and over again. They are the three children of Baron Edmond — James Armand de Rothschild, Maurice Charles de Rothschild, and Alexandrine de Rothschild.

Comparing these lists with the entries in Ettinghausen's list of June 1935, we can see approximately how the collection must have been divided up. Alexandrine reported 45 medieval and illuminated manuscripts as missing. James claimed only nine, all in Hebrew. Since he already had part of his share back in England by 1942 at the latest, when the Seilern Hours was sold, and 27 of his manuscripts are still at Waddesdon, then his share comprised at least 37 items. Maurice reported only eight manuscripts as missing during the War, all of great importance, but he had certainly lodged some items at the Bibliothèque Nationale for safekeeping. As the Ettinghausen list records approximately a hundred items, James may have inherited about 37, Alexandrine about 45, which would leave only eighteen for Maurice. Given the range of quality of the items, this was probably intended as a fair three-way division.

We can begin with the Hebrew manuscripts reported as stolen from James de Rothschild. There are nine in the *Répertoire*, not all necessarily accurately listed for they include a Yemenite scroll dated to the fourth century (possible but exceedingly improbable) and a Hebrew Bible 'orné de nombreuses miniatures' (even less probable, unless 'miniatures' means in this case decoration without pictures). Among others, there is a two-volume Hebrew Bible of the fourteenth century, which must be MS 89 of the Ettinghausen list, there is a 'Livre de prières hébraïques ... sur vélin', and there are three manuscript Haggadot.[14] Some, at least, have reappeared since the War. In 1948, a Dr Fred Towsley Murphy bequeathed an illuminated manuscript Haggadah to Yale University, where it became Beinecke MS Hebrew + 143 and was greatly appreciated.[15] In 1980 a graduate student at Yale, Barbara Hurwitz, drew attention to a pencil number on the flyleaf, 'MS 92'. It thus became apparent that it was not only MS 92 from the Ettinghausen list but that it corresponded exactly with one of the three Haggadot reported on the *Répertoire des Biens Spoliés* as missing during the War from James de Rothschild.[16] After more than 30 years at Yale, the book was duly packed up and sent to James's widow, then still alive, who in turn presented it in 1981 to the Hebrew University of Jerusalem, where it is now MS.Heb.4° 6130.

In May 1950, two years after Dr Murphy's bequest, the bookseller Hugo Streisand of Berlin wrote to the Jewish Theological Seminary in New York offering to sell for $5000 an Italian Hebrew manuscript with over 300 miniatures. The Librarian, Dr Alexander Marx, recognized it as Rothschild MS 24, the famous Rothschild Miscellany, bequeathed to James. After protracted law suits, it too was returned to James de Rothschild. On his death in 1957, it was presented to the Bezalel Museum in Jerusalem, now part of the Israel Museum, as the anonymous (and later disclosed) gift of his widow, where it is now MS 180/51.[17] It is arguably the most important Italian Renaissance manuscript in the Hebrew language, and was published in facsimile in 1989. It is said to have been in gratitude for Dr Marx's help in recovering this supreme manuscript that the Rothschild family in 1966 presented the Jewish Theological College with the so-called Rothschild Mahzor, MS 99 from Ettinghausen's list, illuminated in Florence in 1492.[18]

Though James de Rothschild evidently inherited most of the Hebrew manuscripts, among the most commercially valuable items in the collection, this was evidently offset by the inclusion in the bequests to Alexandrine and Maurice of Western and Near Eastern manuscripts of far greater artistic quality than anything at Waddesdon. One item which jumps off the page in the *Répertoire des Biens Spoliés* is described as 'Heures — Livre d'heures de Jeanne II Reine de Navarre, ms. du XIV^{e}s. . . . 108 miniatures, lettres ornées et bordures à sujets humoristiques'.[19] It was reported by Baronne Alexandrine de Rothschild. The famous and magnificent royal Book of Hours of Joan of Navarre (*d.*1349, daughter of Louis X) had belonged to Lord Ashburnham and thence to Yates Thompson, and in his sale in 1919 had been estimated at £2000 but sold to Quaritch for £11,800, then by far the highest price paid for any illuminated manuscript at auction.[20] Thereafter it simply disappeared from sight. For many decades it was one of the most important 'untraced' works of art.[21] It must be one of the 'Horae' on the Ettinghausen list. Suddenly in the late 1960s it resurfaced in an abbey in Brittany. The tale is recounted by the Parisian auctioneer and friend of the Rothschilds, M. Maurice Rheims.[22] He tells that the long-lost Hours of Joan of Navarre was offered for sale by a priest from an abbey near St-Brieuc in northern Brittany. The priest explained that the book had been found during the War by an army doctor at Berchtesgaden in Austria and that afterwards the doctor had been on a retreat at the abbey and had presented them with his manuscript. When the monastery had been damaged in a storm, the priest took the unidentified manuscript to a bookseller in Rouen to ask if it had any commercial value. Eventually it was referred to the Bibliothèque Nationale and of course was recognized as the supreme missing royal book, reported as stolen from Alexandrine de Rothschild. It was returned to the present Baron, who (M. Rheims relates) generously paid the 40,000 francs needed for the new roof of the abbey and who then, after consulting his aunt Alexandrine, presented the manuscript to the Bibliothèque Nationale. 'I haven't even time to read the Bible', he is reported as saying, 'so I might as well let them have it'. It is now B.N. ms. nouv.acq.lat.3145, and one of the greatest fourteenth-century books.

Another entry in the *Répertoire des Biens Spoliés* reported missing by Alexandrine is oriental, described as 'Abu'l Faze. The Akbar Name ou history of Akbar; ms. indo-persan du XVIᵉs., 162 pages, 39 miniatures . . .'.[23] This is certainly MS 96 on Ettinghausen's list and corresponds to the first volume of the celebrated *Akbar Nama*, or illustrated history of the life and achievements of the Mughal emperor Akbar (1556-1605), made for the Mughal royal library in *c*.1603-5. Both volumes were probably brought to Europe by the dealer Demotte and belonged to Quaritch by 1912. Volume II was sold to Chester Beatty in 1923.[24] Volume I vanished from sight until its reappearance in Switzerland in 1966, when it was bought by the British Library, now Or.MS.12988. Although no provenance is known between 1912 and 1966, it must certainly be assumed that the manuscript was recovered after the War and that its sale in the 1960s was through representatives of Alexandrine de Rothschild.

The same source is doubtless the origin of a group of at least four western illuminated manuscripts sold in the Erasmushaus in Basel, Auktion XXXVIII, 17 June 1964, lots 250-53.[25] They included an extremely rare Book of Hours illuminated in Strasbourg, now in the J. Paul Getty Museum, MS Ludwig IX.16. Two of the four had the book label of James Mayer de Rothschild (1792-1868), the father of Baron Edmond through whose collection they must have come. Three can be matched absolutely with items on the Ettinghausen list and the fourth with probability, and all four are unambiguously on the list of books reported stolen from Alexandrine.[26]

Several years later, on 24 June 1968, there was an undesignated sale in Paris at the Palais Galliéra, *Manuscrits à Peintures*, which caused a sensation.[27] It comprised only twelve manuscripts, but all of the highest quality. There was no reference in the catalogue to their provenance, but it was not long before rumours connected them with the Rothschilds, perhaps with Baroness Alice Charlotte de Rothschild, of Waddesdon.[28] The sale included a unique and quite wonderful manuscript of mystical and visionary Canticles illuminated probably in Thérouanne or St-Omer around 1290, with nearly 300 extraordinary illustrations. It had belonged to the Dukes of Hamilton and then to Walter Sneyd, after whose sale in December 1903 it had been bought by Quaritch for £2500 and had effectively vanished from scholarly sight. As recently as 1980, one scholar wrote, 'Its present whereabouts are, sadly, unknown; it may have been a casualty of the Second World War'.[29] There was a late but hauntingly beautiful Apocalypse with 72 miniatures which had been owned by the Baron Auvray and had disappeared from all records after his sale in 1920.[30] There were some first-class Books of Hours, including an extraordinary one with circular miniatures to be viewed through round apertures cut into the adjacent pages. There were two Florentine Renaissance manuscripts of the most refined quality, one written by the scribe Antonio Sinibaldi and the other by Niccolò Mangona. The final lot in the sale was a bit of an oddity, a large lavish German genealogical manuscript which had last been recorded in 1879 when it had been lent for an exhibition in Paris by Baron Edmond de Rothschild.[31]

Every lot in the sale had pencil inventory numbers, and can be matched with certainty with the Ettinghausen list of June 1935, MSS 8, 12, 22, 28, 33, 36, 37, 62, 75, 77, 95 and 98. One of the lots, an exquisite quarto-sized Book of Hours in the style of Pseudo-Jacquemart, was recognized by Millard Meiss, who had seen the collection in 1936, as having been the property of Alexandrine de Rothschild.[32] Finally, four of the lots in the catalogue appear in the *Répertoire des Biens Spoliés* as items reported by Alexandrine as stolen.[33]

The late Mr E. M. Dring recounted to me that when the sale catalogue reached Quaritch, he actually recognized lot 1, the Canticles, as the long-lost book which his father had sold to Baron Edmond in 1904. He believed, therefore, that he had stumbled on a whole sale of stolen manuscripts, and he telephoned the French Rothschilds with the news, only to learn, as we now know, that the looted manuscripts had come back to the family and that the Rothschilds were now indeed the consignors. There is no doubt that the 1968 sale comprised the large part of the inheritance of Alexandrine de Rothschild.

The 1968 sale achieved some very high prices, including a million francs for the Apocalypse, which was probably then a record price for a manuscript at auction. It came about like this. The lot had been estimated at 150,000/200,000 francs, and Mr H. P. Kraus, who attended the sale in person, wanted it very badly indeed. Until recently, if a work of art was sold by auction in France and was considered to be of national importance, the French Government could pre-empt it immediately at whatever figure it realized in the sale. Therefore when the bidding for the Apocalypse had reached 600,000 francs to M. Marcel Thomas on behalf of the Bibliothèque Nationale, and the hammer was about to fall, Mr Kraus suddenly jumped to his feet and shouted out 'un million!'. There was great commotion and astonishment at such a price and Kraus bought the manuscript – at almost double what it might have cost a few seconds earlier. At such a leap to so unprecedented a level, however, the Bibliothèque Nationale had no chance to exercise their right of pre-emption, and the manuscript was able to leave France quite legally.[34]

Alexandrine must have kept most of her share of Baron Edmond's medieval manuscripts in France, and thus held her principal sale in Paris. Her brother Maurice probably kept his share in Switzerland or elsewhere abroad from after the War. Baron Maurice Charles de Rothschild (1881-1957) was, after his father, the best bibliophile of the family. Sometimes it is difficult to distinguish their separate collections, for Maurice de Rothschild's own library already included the *Très Belles Heures* of the Duc de Berry, a third of that legendary manuscript illuminated first by the Limbourgs around 1404 and then a generation later by the van Eycks. He lodged this and probably other manuscripts at the Bibliothèque Nationale during the War, and gave them his *Très Belles Heures* in 1956, probably in gratitude.[35] It is therefore astonishing to see in the *Répertoire des Biens Spoliés* a manuscript described laconically as 'Heures – Livre d'heures du Duc de Berry, ms. sur vélin de la fin du XIV[e]s. richement décoré de miniatures en camaïeu', reported lost by Baron Maurice de Rothschild.[36] Seldom can so great a work of art ever have been recorded so briefly, for this can only be Baron Edmond's supreme manuscript, the *Belles Heures* of the Duc de Berry, with 94 shimmering full-page miniatures by the Limbourg brothers. It is MS 18 on the Ettinghausen list of Baron Edmond's manuscripts.

The *Belles Heures*, stolen from the Rothschilds, is popularly said to have been found at the end of the War on Munich railway station, but this might equally be a cover story invented in Germany by whoever stole it and needed to explain how he came by it. It is one of a series of outstandingly important medieval manuscripts which were returned to Maurice de Rothschild after the War. The *Belles Heures* was sold directly by Maurice de Rothschild in 1954 to John D. Rockerfeller, Jr., for the Metropolitan Museum in New York and it is now one of the great monuments in The Cloisters (now Cloisters 54.1.1). It was stated openly to have been bought by Edmond de Rothschild in 1880 and to have come to Maurice on Edmond's death.[37] In the same year, the Metropolitan Museum bought from the dealer Jacques Seligman the tiny jewel-like Hours of Jeanne d'Evreux, queen of France, the only manuscript for which there appears to be contemporary evidence to attribute the miniatures to Jean Pucelle, the great early fourteenth-century court painter. The manuscript afterwards passed through the collections of Charles V and, once again, the Duc de Berry. It too was acknowledged publicly as having been inherited by Maurice de Rothschild from his father's collection.[38] The Metropolitan is said to have paid $75,000 for it, an enormous sum for a book in 1954 (now Cloisters 54.1.2).

Baron Maurice himself died in 1957. Around that time a number of supreme oriental illuminated manuscripts appeared on the market, but now with no reference whatsoever to their immediate provenance. If I am correct, they were offered through the New York art dealers Rosenberg and Stiebel. The first Rosenberg had been a neighbour of the Rothschilds in Frankfurt, and the firm had become agents for the Rothschild family both as buyers and, in this case, as sellers. The finest manuscript offered was the vast *Shahnameh* made for Shah Tahmasp of Persia (1524-76), which for over 20 years occupied the greatest artists of Persia and which was finally in 1568 carried by a procession of 34 camels across the Middle East to the library of the sultans of Turkey in the Topkapi. It had 258 illuminated miniatures, and its importance has been compared with that of the Book of Kells. It must have reached Paris by the late nineteenth century. In 1903, Baron Edmond de Rothschild lent it for exhibition at the Musée des Arts Decoratifs. Thereafter it seems to have been withdrawn entirely from sight, slipping for almost 60 years into what Mr Stuart Cary Welch calls mere 'legend'.[39] It may be MS 17 in the Ettinghausen list, 'Persian manuscript, 17th century' but, more importantly, it most certainly is no.398 in the *Répertoire des Biens Spoliés*, described in accurate detail as reported missing by Baron Maurice de Rothschild.[40]

The *Shahnameh* is said to have been priced at $100,000, and it was rejected by several American museums who should have known better and was bought in 1959 by the late Arthur Houghton (1907-90). Mr

Houghton took the extremely difficult decision to dismember it. He gave 78 of its miniatures to the Metropolitan Museum and sold 62 others, both privately and at auction.[41] The bitter-sweet story has an extraordinary and relatively recent twist. The residue of the '*Houghton Shahnameh*', as it is now usually called, with 118 miniatures remaining, was inherited by the Houghton family. It was valued at the time of probate at a reported $13,000,000, but because so many portions of the dismembered book have appeared on the market and are already represented in the richest collections, the corpus of the manuscript is almost unsaleable. Through an astonishing piece of imaginative negotiation with the Iranian Government, the former Rothschild *Shahnameh*, in loose sheets enclosed in nine boxes, was exchanged at Vienna airport on 28 July 1994 for a modern painting, *Woman Three* by the Dutch-American expressionist Willem de Kooning, which had been bought by the late Shah of Persia for his private art collection and which shows a contorted nude woman now considered to be incompatible with Islamic values.[42] Thus the *Shahnameh* has returned to Persia at no cost to the Iranian government, and the Houghton heirs have a painting which is new to the market and is potentially very saleable indeed.

I have heard it suggested that the Rothschilds who inherited manuscripts on Baron Maurice's death in 1957 began with disposing of volumes of Islamic origin because such books seemed inconsistent with possession by a great Jewish family. By the early 1960s, however, a number of overtly Christian prayerbooks began to emerge anonymously on to the market, principally in North America.

Two royal manuscripts were acquired by the Cleveland Museum of Art in 1963-4, both apparently through Rosenberg and Stiebel. The first is the Hours of Queen Isabel la Católica, one of the most refined of Ghent/Bruges manuscripts, illuminated around 1500 for Isabel of Castile (1451-1504) who, with her husband Ferdinand of Aragon, was joint ruler of united Spain and patron of Christopher Columbus. The lovely Book of Hours was almost unknown when the Museum bought it through the Leonard C. Hanna Jr. Bequest in 1963, but was cited briefly but unambiguously as being in the Rothschild collection in Paris in 1908 and in 1924.[43] The second is the Hours of Charles the Noble. It was bought by Cleveland through the Mr and Mrs William H. Marlatt Fund in 1964. Charles the Noble (1361-1425) was King of Navarre and his opulent Book of Hours was made in Paris, *c.*1405, by an Italian artist who had also worked for the Duc de Berry.[44] Millard Meiss recalled having seen this manuscript on his privileged visit to the Rothschild house in Paris in 1936.[45] It was reported by Maurice de Rothschild to the *Répertoire des Biens Spoliés*,[46] and had been recovered by 1949 when it was exhibited at the Bibliothèque Nationale.[47]

In approximately 1968, at least three Rothschild manuscripts were sold privately to H. P. Kraus through a New York attorney. As recounted by Kraus, when the agent was asked about the possible Rothschild origin of two of the books, he replied 'I am instructed to keep the ownership strictly confidential'.[48] These two, bought for a combined total of $200,000, were the Froissart of Edward IV and the Hours of Claude de France. The Froissart belonged to Baron Edmond by 1879 and is MS 3 on the Ettinghausen list.[49] The tiny Hours of Claude de France is one of two eponymous works by the important Renaissance illuminator now known as the Master of Claude de France, made for Claude (1499-1524), daughter of Louis XII and wife of François I. It had been in England in the early nineteenth century, was engraved for Dibdin's *Bibliographical Decameron* in 1817, and disappeared after 1864.[50] A third manuscript which came to Kraus and was sold by him to Yale in 1968 is the Missal in French with over a hundred large miniatures, and the spuriously added arms of Charles VI of France and Henry V of England. It had been in the Hoe sale of 1911, and was probably MS 13 in the Ettinghausen list. It is now MS 425 in the Beinecke Library.[51]

Probably the most famous manuscript discovery in the 1960s is that of the Hours of Catherine of Cleves. The story is well-known but merits re-telling because its connection with Edmond de Rothschild is not so well-known. The Book of Hours itself is generally regarded as the most important Dutch manuscript in existence, made for Catherine of Cleves (1417-76), Duchess of Guelders and Countess of Zutphen. One volume was in the library of the dukes of Arenberg, which was bought *en bloc* in 1957 by Kraus, who sold the Catherine of Cleves immediately on receiving it for $80,000 to Alastair Bradley Martin. Then, in 1963, to the absolute astonishment of the scholarly world, another manuscript claimed to be the Hours of Catherine of Cleves was offered to the Pierpont Morgan Library, 'through a New York art dealer who had received it on consignment from a private owner in Europe'.[52] The dealer must have been Rosenberg and Stiebel. Millard Meiss, thinking about the manuscript 30 years after the event, remembered it from the Rothschild library.[53] On the *Répertoire des Biens Spoliés* is the shortest possible entry reported by Baron Maurice de Rothschild. It appears simply as 'Heures, Livre d'heures de Catherine de Clèves' and is located among manuscripts to which no dates could be assigned.[54] This great book must have gone on a hitherto unsuspected excursion into Germany or eastern Europe.

What seems to have happened is that the very bulky but slightly imperfect Hours of Catherine of Cleves was on the market in Paris in the mid-nineteenth century. A dealer, probably Techener, finding it hard to sell, took it apart and reassembled the leaves into two apparently integral books, marked both as *the* Hours of Catherine of Cleves, and sold one to the Dukes of Arenberg and one to the Rothschilds. The two parts are now again companion volumes in the Morgan Library, M.917 (the Rothschild volume) and M.945 (the Arenberg volume, added to the Library in 1970).

Thus, gradually, there is emerging some idea of the extraordinary quality and variety of the manuscript collection of Baron Edmond de Rothschild. Even allowing for items not identifiable on the *Répertoire des Biens Spoliés*, we can probably point with some confidence to recognizable records of not far off 80 illuminated manuscripts once in the library. There are other manuscripts which have appeared in recent decades and which seem to be candidates for having Rothschild provenances but which have eluded my attempts to pin them down.[55] Books of Hours in particular, of which Baron Edmond owned at least 49 examples, are the most difficult to match up with the Ettinghausen inventory and we must assume that great books like the Hours of Joan of Navarre, Charles the Noble and Catherine of Cleves are on that list simply as 'Horae'. There are, furthermore, books both on that list and on the *Répertoire des Biens Spoliés* which cannot easily be matched with known books, and which may still belong to the family[56] or may be untraced still somewhere in eastern Europe. A Florentine Book of Hours apparently signed by the scribe Antonio Sinibaldi, for example, was in Baron Edmond's library in Paris in 1914 and does not appear to be known now.[57] The *Répertoire* of missing manuscripts includes a fourteenth-century Petrarch, a medieval Gospel Book ('Ms. ancien de style gothique' – a tantalizing entry), and many Books of Hours which sound quite lovely, including one, which ought to be recognizable, of miniature size (60mm × 40mm) in a tooled Renaissance binding with enamel and gold clasps formed like two entwined hands.[58] Another is the Agnese portolan atlas made in Venice for Philip II of Spain as the son of the Emperor Charles V. It was last recorded in the Spitzer catalogue in 1892, is MS 25 on the Ettinghausen inventory, and was reported as lost in the War by Alexandrine de Rothschild.[59] That would be a very pleasing association copy – the atlas of the world made for the monarch who owned nearly half of it.

It is difficult to know how to assess Baron Edmond de Rothschild in the context of antiquaries and circles of learning. There is no suggestion of bookish parties of fellow enthusiasts hunched up excitedly over rare black-letter discoveries in a dusty library late at night, the sort of agreeable image conjured (for me, anyway) by the word 'antiquary'. It would be easier to judge the Rothschilds in the context of the Duc de Berry or Philip II or Catherine the Great. Baron Edmond was the grandson of the first great Rothschild banker, Mayer Amschel Rothschild (1743-1812), of Frankfurt, who sent his five sons out to establish the family bank in the principal cities of Europe. The youngest son, James Mayer de Rothschild (1792-1868), was sent to Paris and within one generation he was the richest man in France. He was a flamboyant, cultivated bon-viveur, built the great house at Ferrières, and began the manuscript collection. There are nine medieval manuscripts at Waddesdon, for example, which have his circular ticket printed in blue, 'Bibliothèque du Baron J. de Rothschild' around a coronet. Some of his manuscripts were bound with his arms on the sides. His books were generally very late medieval, bright, showy, and perhaps not especially expensive. He died in November 1868 when his younger son Edmond, who probably inherited all the manuscripts, was only 23 years old

Baron Edmond was clearly a man of extraordinary learning, and with a passion for the history of art. He must have seized on the manuscripts as the most intellectually satisfying point of intersection between books and painting. Edmond began collecting very early. He had bought his vast Aesop with 147 miniatures by 1872 and the equally huge Christine de Pisan with 115 miniatures in 1873.[60] These are serious and sophisticated purchases for a man of well under 30. Many manuscripts were certainly bought in the 1870s and 1880s (the *Belles Heures* was acquired in 1880, for example) and probably most of the collection had been assembled by the early 1890s, with isolated and extremely grand additions until at least as late as 1920.

The possession of overtly Christian manuscripts is perhaps unusual in a collector who was the virtual world leader in the promotion of Zionism, and may partly explain his reluctance to share his manuscripts

Fig.1. Baron Edmond de Rothschild (1845-1934). Photographed in the 1920s. *Reproduced by courtesy of the National Trust.*

with fellow antiquaries later in life. By soon after 1900, Baron Edmond seems to have withdrawn his collection entirely from public knowledge. He gave two Hebrew books to the Staatbibliothek in Frankfurt before 1920,[61] and he owned about a dozen medieval Hebrew manuscripts, but no more than in any other branch of manuscript studies. Several contributors to the present symposium on antiquaries have touched on the religious motives of book collectors, which are understandable, but to move quite outside into other cultures shows a connoisseurship based on quality which is strikingly modern. Even more extraordinary than buying Books of Hours is that Baron Edmond purchased Islamic illuminated manuscripts, and he owned at least five outstanding Persian or Mughal manuscripts. In this he was far ahead of contemporary collecting taste, even with the French fashion for orientalism.

Baron Edmond preferred books of the late Middle Ages. In this he was quite different from his contemporary and fellow-banker Pierpont Morgan who was buying up splendid Carolingian and romanesque books, or Lord Crawford or even Yates Thompson, Chester Beatty or Henry Walters. Probably no book in the Rothschild library (apart from Hebrew manuscripts) was older than the mid-thirteenth century, and most were fifteenth- or even early sixteenth-century. All (except Hebrew books again) had miniatures, and all were in pristine condition. He admired books of royal provenances. Baron Edmond, like many collectors, built actively on strengths: when he owned or had inherited one outstanding book he gathered others related to it and sometimes even had them bound virtually to match on the shelves. He had little clutches of manuscripts in the style or hands of Jean Pucelle, the Limbourgs, Jean Bourdichon and Simon Bening, and must have looked out for these names. When faced with a possible purchase, he was in a position to pay almost any price. By no means all of his books were of the highest quality, for the infilling of the shelves around the absolutely supreme books inevitably brought in books which look poor in comparison. The scattering of the collection, including the arrival of some of these lesser books at Waddesdon, probably gives a very different impression to what it would have done in Paris around the turn of the century.

By now I hope that Baron Edmond de Rothschild is beginning to emerge as a medieval manuscript collector probably without parallel in the history of antiquarianism and circles of learning. The melting away of his collection, through the terrible years of the War and through generous gifts and discreet sales by his heirs, has almost lost us the knowledge that the library ever existed. But this one man owned the Books of Hours of Joan of Navarre, of Jeanne d'Evreux, of the Duc de Berry, of Charles the Noble, of Catherine of Cleves, of Claude de France, of Isabel the Catholic, and part of that of Henry VII. He had the Rothschild Canticles, the Rothschild Miscellany in Hebrew, the Seilern Hours, the Portolan of Philip II, the Froissart of Edward IV, the Cloisters Apocalypse, Akbar's copy of the *Akbar Nama* and Shah Tahmasp's *Shahnameh*. By today's commercial standards these dozen and a half books alone would probably exceed the entire libraries of every antiquary discussed in this whole symposium put together. Financial value is by no means everything, but simply as a book collector Baron Edmond de Rothschild probably has no equal.

References

1. L. M. J. Delaissé, James Marrow and John de Wit, *The James A. de Rothschild Collection at Waddesdon Manor, Illuminated Manuscripts*, London and Fribourg, 1977.
2. *Times Literary Supplement*, 28 July 1978, p.871.
3. R. Schilling, *Burlington Magazine*, LXXX-LXXXI, 1942, pp.194-7.
4. M. Meiss, *French Painting in the Time of Jean de Berry, The Limbourgs and their Contemporaries*, London and New York, 1974, p.330, with bibliography.
5. The visit is mentioned in Meiss, *French Painting in the Time of Jean de Berry, The Late Fourteenth Century and the Patronage of the Duke*, London and New York, 1967, pp.323 and 396, n.16, and in his *French Painting in the Time of Jean de Berry, The Boucicaut Master*, London and New York, 1968, p.148, n.20, 'the owner would not permit any photographs'.
6. *Catalogue des Vases, Colonnes, Tables de Marbres rares . . . qui composent le Cabinet de feu M. Le Duc d'Aumont*, Paris, 1782, extra-illustrated by Charles-German de St-Aubin; sold in the Pichon sale, 3 May 1897, lot 525, and then as the property of Stig Wilton, Sotheby's, 13 February 1951, lot 368, to Zahle, now privately owned in Paris.
7. M. L. Ettinghausen, *Rare Books and Royal Collectors*, New York, 1966, p.53.
8. *2*, Giron le Courtois; *3*, Froissart's Chronicles; *4*, Aesop; *5*, Histoire grecque et romaine; *6*, Christine de Pisan; *8*, Genealogy of the Derrer Family; *10*, Epîtres à l'usage de Versailles; *11*, Livre des Evangiles à l'usage de Versailles, 1725; *12*, Livre des trois vertus; *13*, Missale gallicanum; *14*, Album d'oiseaux, 17th century; *15*, Incunable: Printed pentateuch on vellum, Bologna, 1482; *16*, Hebrew Bible with Mazoretic text and Halftaroth; *17*, Persian manuscript, 17th century; *18*, Hours of Duke de Berry; *19*, Horae: Anne de Bretagne; *20*, Paris Missal, 16th century; *21*, Horae; *22*, Horae; *23*, Horae; *25*, Portulan of Charles V; *26*, Couronnement d'Anne de Bretagne; *27*, Italian Horae; *28*, Italian Horae, Florence, c.1490; *30*, Horae, Flemish; *31*, Horae, red velvet; *32*, Dutch Horae; *33*, Antiphonal, Miniature by Clovio ?; *34*, Plans de Picardie; *36*, Naldus: Carmen; *37*, Horae; *38*, Horae; *39*, Horae; *40*, French Horae; *41*, French Horae; *42*, French Horae; *43*, French Horae; *44*, Dutch Horae; *45*, Horae;

46, Fragment; *47*, Horae, Flemish; *48*, French Horae; *49*, English Horae; *50*, Horae; *51*, Dutch Horae; *52*, French Horae; *53*, French Horae; *54*, Horae; *55* French Horae; *56*, Horae; *57*, Biblia latina; *58*, French Bible; *59*, Horae; *60*, Italian Horae; *61*, Horae; *62*, French Horae, Catherine de Medici binding; *63*, 13 miniatures; *64*, Parisian Horae; *65*, French Horae; *66*, French Horae; *67*, Dutch Horae; *68*, French Horae; *69*, Set of 11 miniatures; *70*, Fragment; *71*, Italian Horae; *72*, French Horae; *73*, Rhenish prayers; *74*, Horae; *75*, Biblia sacra; *76*, Paradisus precum; *77*, Horae de duchesse de Berry; *78*, Dutch Horae; *79*, Horae; *80*, Horae; *81*, Horae; *82*, Office en français; *83*, German prayers; *85*, Ovid metamorphoses, 1632; *86*, Toison d'Or; *87*, Géographie du Comte de Provence, 1766; *88*, Prussian uniforms; *89*, Hebrew Ms., 2 vols.; *90*, French Horae, Dance of Death decoration; *92*, Hagadah; 94, Ashburnham MS; *95*, Apocalypse; *96*, Akbar-Namah, Persian MS, 16th century; *97bis*, French Psalter; *98*, Cantica canticorum; *99*, Hebrew prayers, Florence, 1492; *99bis*, Complete Hebrew Bible, 14th or 15th century; *100*, Receuil de 10 miniatures persanes; *101*, Indian album: 28 miniatures, 18th century; *102*, Album of Indo-Persian miniatures.

9. H. P. Kraus, *A Rare Book Saga*, London, 1979, p.292.

10. Berès, *Manuscrits & Enluminures du onzième au dix-huitième siècle*, 1974, no.21, bought from the Esmerian sale; Kraus, *Illuminated Manuscripts*, cat.159, 1981, no.23, and cat.188, 1991, no.34, bought from Haus der Bücher, Basel, 27 September 1978, lot 345. The former volume had been exhibited in Paris in 1879 as the property of Baron Edmond de Rothschild (Baron Alphonse de Ruble, *Notice des principaux livres manuscrits et imprimés qui on fait parti de l'exposition de l'Art Ancien au Trocadéro*, Paris, 1879, p.109, no.265). The books are a matching pair of vast royal Lectionaries, made for the chapel of Queen Marie Leczinska at Versailles, written probably by Jean-Pierre Rousselet, illustrated with extraordinary flower paintings, and later bound by Thouvenin, *c.*1820.

11. Sotheby's, 18 June 1991, lot 124, the Missal of Etienne de Longwy, Mâcon, *c.*1490, has 'MS 13' in pencil on the flyleaf; it had previously been sold at Sotheby's, 10 July 1967, lot 100, and was subsequently H. P. Kraus, cat.193, 1993, no.12. Slight caution is needed here, for MS 13 could also be identifiable as New Haven, Yale University, Beinecke Library MS 425 (see below, n.51). Sotheby's, 3 July 1984, lot 89, a Book of Hours by the Master of Guillebert de Mets, *c.*1440, has 'MS 32' in pencil on the flyleaf; it was subsequently reproduced in C. de Hamel, *A History of Illuminated Manuscripts*, 2 ed., 1994, p.187, pl.166, as 'Switzerland, private collection'; a missing miniature from the same manuscript was Sotheby's, 2 December 1986, lot 12.

12. The Netherlands, private collection (C. de Hamel, *Catalogue of Manuscripts and Miniatures*, Hilversum, 1982, pp.42-9), a Book of Hours with twelve full-page miniatures; it has the earlier booklabel of Baron James Mayer de Rothschild (1792-1868), Baron Edmond's father, and a small circular stamp in black, 'Coll. H de R'.

13. Commandement en Chef Français en Allemagne, Groupe Français du Conseil de Controle, *Répertoire des Biens Spoliés en France durant la Guerre 1939-1945*, VII, *Archives, Manuscrits et Livres Rares*, Berlin, n.d. [1948].

14. *Ibid.*, p.29 (nos.328, 339 and 335) and p.54 (nos.661-3).

15. W. Cahn and J. Marrow, 'Medieval and Renaissance Manuscripts at Yale: A Selection', *The Yale University Library Gazette*, LII, 1978, pp.235-6, no.61, with bibliography.

16. *Yale News*, 2 October 1980, pp.1 and 6; *The New York Times*, 5 October 1980; T. Gollin, 'The Case of Murphy's Haggadah', *Yale Alumni Magazine*, December 1980, pp.18-19. There is no suggestion that Dr Murphy had known of the book's history, and nor had he nor any member of his family served in the army during the War. The manuscript has the stamp of William V. Black which might be a clue as to how it entered Murphy's possession.

17. B. Richler, *Guide to Hebrew Manuscript Collections*, Jerusalem, 1994, pp.164-5. The manuscript has been disbound and there is no longer a number on the flyleaf or inside the cover; in the Ettinghausen list there is no number between MS 23 and MS 25.

18. New York, Jewish Theological Seminary Mic.8892, also known as the Rothschild Siddur; cf. E.M. Cohen, *The Rothschild Mahzor*, New York, 1983.

19. *Répertoire des Biens Spoliés*, p.30 (no.344).

20. Sotheby's, 3 June 1919, lot 5.

21. E.g., K. Morand, *Jean Pucelle*, Oxford, 1962, pp.48-49, 'Location Unknown'; Meiss, *Late Fourteenth Century*, pp.20, 87, 104, etc., 'Whereabouts unknown'.

22. M. Rheims, *The Glorious Obsession*, tr. P. Evans, London, 1980, pp.224-7.

23. *Répertoire des Biens Spoliés*, p.33 (no.386).

24. MS 3; cf. L. Y. Leach, *Mughal and Other Indian Paintings from the Chester Beatty Library*, I, London, 1995, pp.232-300. Note that the volume listed in the *Répertoire* is mostly entered in English, presumably reflecting the Quaritch description from which it was bought.

25. Haus der Bücher, Basel, and L'Art Ancien, Zurich; the same auctioneers later offered the Versailles Lectionary, cited in n.10 above.

26. Lot 250 (Book of Hours, Use of Sarum, 25 full-page miniatures, Southern Netherlands for the English market, mid-fifteenth century) = J. M. de Rothschild no.10; Ettinghausen list MS 49; *Répertoire*, p.32 (no.373); afterwards Kraus, cat.117 (1967), no.11; Hamburg, Hauswedell, 12-13 February 1971, lot 5844; Stuttgart, private collection MS 32, eliminated in 1991 by exchange with J. Günther.
Lot 251 (Book of Hours, Use of the Johannites, 19 full-page miniatures, Strasbourg, early sixteenth century) = J. M. de Rothschild no.21; Ettinghausen list MS 73, *Répertoire*, p.55 (no.676); afterwards Kraus, cat.117 (1967), no.18, now Malibu, J. Paul Getty Museum MS Ludwig IX.16.
Lot 252 (Book of Hours, 18 large miniatures, Paris or Rouen, c.1500) = Ettinghausen list MS 40; *Répertoire*, p.55 (no.680).
Lot 253 (fragment with six large and four small miniatures from a Book of Hours) = 'vermutlich' J. M. de Rothschild, perhaps Ettinghausen list MS 70, *Répertoire*, p.54 (no.669).

27. Rheims et Laurin, and Mme. J. Vidal-Mégret. Three sales of autographs took place at about that time, all rumoured to come from the Rothschilds, but I cannot confirm whether or not they were consigned from the same source, *Précieux Manuscrits et Lettres Autographes*, Drouot, Rheims and Laurin, 29 May 1968, 26 February 1969 and 15 December 1969.

28. Kraus, *Rare Book Saga*, p.290.

29. R. W. Pfaff, *Montague Rhodes James*, London, 1980, p.196. Quaritch commissioned a special catalogue from M. R. James but sold the book in 1904 while the catalogue

was still in proof; cf. now J. F. Hamburger, *The Rothschild Canticles, Art and Mysticism in Flanders and the Rhineland, circa 1300*, New Haven and London, 1990.

30. Lot 2, previously sold in Tours, 9 June 1920, lot 203 (P. Lauer, 'Bibliographie des publications relatives aux manuscrits à peintures, parues de 1913 à 1920', *Société français de Reproduction de Manuscrits à Peintures*, 1914-1920, p.175); cf. now F. Deuchler, J. M. Hoffeld and H. Nickel, *The Cloisters Apocalypse*, New York, 1971.

31. A. de Ruble, *Notice . . . de l'exposition de l'Art Ancien au Trocadéro*, 1879, pp.101-2, no.299.

32. Meiss, *The Limbourgs and their Contemporaries*, p.359.

33. Lot 1 (Canticles, 46 full-page miniatures, Artois, late thirteenth century) = Ettinghausen list MS 98; now New Haven, Yale University, Beinecke MS 404.

Lot 2 (Apocalypse, 72 large miniatures, region of Switzerland, early fourteenth century) = Ettinghausen list MS 95; now New York, Metropolitan Museum of Art, Cloisters Collection.

Lot 3 (Bible, 82 historiated initials, central France, mid-thirteenth century) = Ettinghausen list MS 75; *Répertoire*, p.53 (no.647); now Germany, private collection, MS 15.

Lot 4 (Book of Hours, Use of Paris, 16 large miniatures, Paris, early fifteenth century) = Ettinghausen list MS 22; now private collection.

Lot 5 (Book of Hours, Use of Paris, 11 large miniatures, Paris, early fifteenth century) = Ettinghausen list MS 62; *Répertoire*, p.33 (no.391).

Lot 6 (Christine de Pisan, *Livre des Trois Vertus*, four miniatures, mid-fifteenth century) = Ettinghausen list MS 12; *Répertoire*, p.55 (no.685); now New Haven, Yale University, Beinecke MS 427.

Lot 7 (Book of Hours, 6 full-page miniatures, Florence, late fifteenth century) = Ettinghausen list MS 28; afterwards Sotheby's, 13 July 1977, lot 90; now Geneva, Comites Latentes MS 191.

Lot 8 (Antiphoner, very large historiated initial, Rome, c.1500) = Ettinghausen list MS 33; afterwards Kraus, *Monumenta* (1974), no.42; now Malibu, J. Paul Getty Museum, MS Ludwig VI.3.

Lot 9 (Book of Hours, 16 circular miniatures, probably Tours, c.1500) = Ettinghausen list MS 37; afterwards Kraus, *Monumenta* (1974), no.41; now private collection.

Lot 10 (Naldus de Naldis, *Carmen Nuptiale*, Florence, c.1503) = Ettinghausen list MS 36; afterwards Paris, Bernard Malle (according to P. O. Kristeller, *Iter Italicum, Accendunt Alia Itinera*, III, 1983, p.340); Breslauer, 1985; now Germany, private collection MS 43 (stolen, 19/20 February 1996).

Lot 11 (Book of Hours, Use of Paris, 15 large and 15 small miniatures, early sixteenth century) = Ettinghausen list MS 77; now New Haven, Yale University, Beinecke MS 375.

Lot 12 (Genealogy of the Derrer family, Nuremberg, 1626-1711) = Ettinghausen list MS 8; *Répertoire*, p.37 (no.439); now Malibu, J. Paul Getty Museum MS. Ludwig XIII.12.

34. Kraus, *Rare Book Saga*, pp.290-1.

35. B.N. ms. nouv.acq.lat.3093; cf. now E. König, *Die Très Belles Heures de Notre-Dame des Herzogs von Berry, Kommentar*, Luzern, 1992.

36. *Répertoire*, p.30 (no.343).

37. E.g., J. J. Rorimer, *The Belles Heures of Jean, Duke of Berry, Prince of France*, New York, 1958, p.[4].

38. J. J. Rorimer, *The Hours of Jeanne d'Évreux, Queen of France*, New York, 1957, pp.5-6, 'This extraordinary manuscript came to the New York market in 1953 from the collection of Baron Maurice de Rothschild and was acquired for The Cloisters the following year'; C. U. Faye and W. H. Bond, *Supplement to the Census of Medieval and Renaissance Manuscripts in the United States and Canada*, New York, 1962, p.328, state that it had come to Maurice from his father Edmond de Rothschild.

39. S. C. Welch, *A King's Book of Kings, The Shah-Nameh of Shah Tahmasp*, New York, 1972, p.17.

40. *Répertoire*, p.34 (no.398).

41. Christie's, *Seven Folios from the Houghton Shahnameh*, 17 November 1976; Agnew's, *Persian Miniatures, An Exhibition of Seventeen Pages from the Houghton Shahnameh*, July-August 1979; Christie's, *Fourteen Folios from the Houghton Shahnameh*, 11 October 1988; others were sold privately through Colnaghi's; four acquired through Agnew's in 1977 by the British Rail Pension Fund reappeared at Sotheby's, 23 April 1996, lot 11-14. Leaves are now in many major collections, including the Los Angeles County Museum of Art, the Museum of Fine Arts in Richmond (Virginia), the Staatliche Museen Preussicher Kulturbesitz in Berlin, and in the David Collection in Copenhagen. The decision to break up the greatest extant Persian manuscript has not been without its critics, including E. Munro, 'How to Mangle a Masterpiece, The Sad Story of the Houghton Shahnameh', *Saturday Review*, 27 October 1979, pp.21-6; and S. Melikian, 'A Persian Tale of Splendor and Destruction', *Herald Tribune*, 28 September 1979.

42. *The Independent*, 4 August 1994.

43. G. Coggiola, *Das Breviarium Grimani in der Bibliothek von San Marco in Venedig, Seine Geschichte und seine Kunst*, Leiden and Leipzig, 1908, p.201, and E. Michel, 'Le Bréviaire de la collection Mayer van den Bergh à Anvers', *Gazette des Beaux-Arts*, LXVI, 1924, p.202, both references which I owe to P. M. de Winter, 'A Book of Hours of Queen Isabel la Católica', *Bulletin of The Cleveland Museum of Art*, LXVII, 1981, pp.342-427. Dr de Winter describes it as 'a Book of Hours of extraordinary quality which for many years had been the property of Baron Edmond de Rothschild in Paris' (p.342) and notes, 'The volume, as far as I can gather, was in the collection of Anselm de Rothschild in Frankfurt-am-Main from which it passed to that of Edmond de Rothschild in Paris' (p.421, n.2), which may represent a conflation of two books. A pencil inscription inside the upper cover, beginning 'M21', might link this with MS 21, 'Horae', on the Ettinghausen list. The Book of Hours itself is now CMA.63.256.

44. W. D. Wixom, 'The Hours of Charles the Noble', *Bulletin of The Cleveland Museum of Art*, LII, 1965, pp.50-83.

45. Meiss, *Late Fourteenth Century*, p.323.

46. *Répertoire*, p.30 (no.342).

47. J. Porcher, *Manuscrits et livres précieux retrouvés en allemagne*, Paris, 1949, p.9, no.2.

48. Kraus, *Rare Book Saga*, p.292.

49. A. de Ruble, *Notice . . . de l'exposition de l'Art Ancien au Trocadéro*, 1879, p.32, no.53; it was afterwards Kraus, *Monumenta* (1974), no.40, priced at $385,000, and is now Malibu, J. Paul Getty Museum, MS Ludwig XIII.7. The manuscript has 25 large and

39 small miniatures, and appears to be a stray volume from the English royal library last recorded in the inventory of 1535.

50. Kraus, *Monumenta* (1974), p.111, no.44, from 'a member of the Rothschild family', and C. Sterling, *The Master of Claude, Queen of France, A Newly Defined Miniaturist*, New York, 1975. It was described by T. F. Dibdin, *Bibliographical Decameron*, I, London, 1817, pp.clxxx-clxxxi, and was last recorded in the George Daniel sale, Sotheby's, 24 July 1864, lot 1177, £285 to Butler. It is now in the same private collection as the Book of Hours cited above, n.33, lot 9.

51. The identification with MS 13, first credibly made by James Marrow (*The Yale University Library Gazette*, LII, 1978, p.254), is complicated by the occurrence of the same pencil number in the Missal described above, n.11.

52. J. Plummer, *The Hours of Catherine of Cleves*, New York, 1966, p.10. No provenance at all for this volume between the 1850s and 1963 is given by H. L. M. Defoer, A. S. Korteweg and W. C. M. Wüstefeld, *The Golden Age of Dutch Manuscript Painting*, Utrecht and New York, 1989, pp.152-60.

53. *Boucicaut Master*, p.148, n.20, as above, n.5.

54. *Répertoire*, p.54 (no.667).

55. The Prayerbook of Albrecht of Brandenburg has been on and off my list several times (it is currently off again). This masterpiece by Simon Bening, now Malibu, J. Paul Getty Museum, MS Ludwig IX.19, disappeared after being sold for 28,000 francs in Paris in 1869, and it reappeared in the Bodmer Library in the 1950s. Probably it belonged to the Viennese Rothschilds. Another, which has haunted me since I first saw it in Munich in 1975, is the Spinola Hours, now also in the J. Paul Getty Museum, MS Ludwig IX.18, which has an absolute black hole of non-provenance: it is, however, absolutely not on the *Répertoire des Biens Spoliés*. Two first-class Books of Hours sold at Sotheby's, 6th December 1983, lots 83 and 86, were consigned by the same owner as Sotheby's, 3 July 1984, lot 89, which was certainly from the library of Baron Edmond (see above, n.11); the former had last been offered for sale in Paris in 1869 (A. Bachelin, *Description du Livre d'Heures du prieuré de Saint-Lô de Rouen*), which is consistent with items acquired by Baron Edmond, but I can see no trace of pencil numbers in either book.

56. Not long ago, I saw propped up in the drawing-room of a close relative of the Rothschilds in Paris the presumed dedication miniature from Bourdichon's so-called Hours of Henry VII, cited in 1933 as belonging to Baron Edmond de Rothschild (D. MacGibbon, *Jean Bourdichon, A Court Painter of the Fifteenth Century*, Glasgow, 1933, p.104; it is recorded as untraced by J. Backhouse, 'French Manuscript Illumination, 1450-1530' in T. Kren, ed., *Renaissance Painting in Manuscripts, Treasures from the British Library*, New York, 1983, p.167, fig.21f, and by W. M. Voelkle and R. S. Wieck, *The Bernard H. Breslauer Collection of Manuscript Illuminations*, New York, 1992, p.78). It had been sold at Sotheby's, 14 July 1920, lot 67, £1000 to Agnew.

57. P. D'Ancona, *La Miniatura Fiorentina (Secoli XI-XVI)*, II, *Catalogo Descrittivo*, Florence, 1914, p.886, no.1716, cites two similar books in the collection, one known to be by Sinibaldi and one with the arms of Baronicelli-Bandini; the latter was lot 7 in the 1968 sale (see above, n.33, and is, in fact by Sinibaldi too, though unsigned), but the former does not seem to be recognizable among known Sinibaldi manuscripts in A. C. de la Mare, 'New Research on Humanistic Scribes in Florence', in A.

Garzelli, ed., *Miniatura Fiorentina del Rinascimento, 1440-1525, Un Primo Censimento*, I, Florence, 1985, pp.484-7.

58. *Répertoire*, pp.30 (no.353), 53 (no.654) and 55 (no.684).

59. A. Moliner in *La collection Spitzer*, V, Paris, 1892, pp.143-4, no.30; *Répertoire*, p.33 (no.387).

60. The Aesop, Waddesdon MS 15, was bound for Edmond by Trautz-Bauzonnet in 1872 (Delaissé *et al.*, p.311; many other manuscripts were re-bound for him by Trautz, *d.*1879, or by Tibaron, *d.*1885). The Christine de Pisan, Waddesdon MS 8, was apparently bought by F[atout] through Quaritch for Edmond at the Perkins sale in June 1873 (*ibid.*, p.170). Note that both are secular texts, which may have appealed to a young Jewish collector.

61. Richler, *Hebrew Manuscript Collections*, 1994, pp.55 and 165. They were afterwards ceded to a Jewish collector in New York as part of the reparations at the end of the Second World War.

The library of the Society of Antiquaries of London: acquiring antiquaries' books over three centuries

BERNARD NURSE

THE SOCIETY OF ANTIQUARIES OF LONDON was founded in 1707 and has a continuous history since 1717; it is therefore the second oldest learned society in Britain after the Royal Society.[1] Until the middle of the eighteenth century, the Antiquaries met in rented apartments or, more often, in the Mitre Tavern, off Fleet Street, where there was little room for books. On Christmas Eve 1718 the Director was ordered 'to provide us a box to lay up the books in', and the first purchase was Strype's 1720 edition of Stow's *Survey of London*.[2] Since then the library has been built up by Fellows for their own use and that of other scholars. Until the twentieth century probably most items were acquired by gift. The library therefore reflects the interests of past Fellows in all branches of antiquarian studies, including topography, heraldry, archaeology and architectural history. By 1735, Kortholt was able to speak of 'a diminutive library whose shelves abound with choice books'.[3]

However, a voluntary association was unable to receive bequests, and in particular, the bequest in 1749 by Lord Coleraine of his prints and drawings. The royal charter granted in 1751 was designed to overcome this problem by establishing a corporate body which could hold property in perpetuity. The charter also set out the object of the Society, which was to encourage the study and knowledge of antiquity and the history of former times. In practice, such a broad collecting policy was impossible to fulfil in any comprehensive way by the voluntary efforts of a small society. A tavern was no longer thought to be a suitable place for a chartered society to meet and in 1753 a former coffee house in Chancery Lane was rented, providing a secure home for the first time. In 1754, the Society's newly created governing body, the Council, ordered

that proper shelves and drawers, under the direction of the Secretaries, be erected for their immediate reception and of such other prints, plates, books, pamphlets and papers as now are, or hereafter may become the property of this

Society; and assigned the large room of this house up two pairs of stairs towards the street, for that purpose.[4]

The fellowship had grown from 23 in 1717 to about 150; expansion of the collections was now possible, and the first important gifts were received. The 1200 prints and drawings bequeathed by Lord Coleraine came in 1754.[5] In 1756 several thousand early broadsides and proclamations were given by a lawyer, Thomas Hollis, including many rare proclamations formerly in the collection of Humphrey Dyson (d.1631). The Hollis gift formed the major part of the Society's extensive collections in this area. In 1852, Robert Lemon divided all that had been received by this time into broadsides and proclamations, put them in chronological order and bound them into volumes.[6] Charles Lyttleton, Bishop of Carlisle and President from 1765 until his death in 1768, bequeathed about 90 printed books and manuscripts, which included the finest illuminated manuscript in the Society's possession, the thirteenth-century Lindsey Psalter.[7] However, one sizeable bequest of works on English history that was lost to Oxford was that of the great collector and outstanding Fellow, Richard Rawlinson. He changed his will in 1754, the year before he died, after his failure to be elected to Council because of his Jacobite sympathies.[8]

The Society soon outgrew its rooms in Chancery Lane, and was fortunate to be able to move in 1781 to the Strand front of Somerset House. This had been newly built on a grand scale to designs by Sir William Chambers to house the Royal Academy, the Royal Society and the Society of Antiquaries by order of their royal patron, George III. The work of the chartered societies in encouraging learning was seen to benefit the public and justify the provision of suitable premises from the public purse. Adequate space for libraries was an important element of Chambers's designs. The rooms are now occupied by the galleries of the Courtauld Institute.

The Society was becoming comparatively large with nearly 400 members, and commissioned some valuable work recording historic buildings, such as the Palace of Westminster. The first catalogues of books and manuscripts were published in 1816.[9] Exchanges of publications with British and foreign societies were instituted, and now number over 200, accounting for many of the long runs of journals held. However it failed to attract any notable gifts until 1828 when Thomas Kerrich, the Librarian of Cambridge University, bequeathed most of the early portraits which adorn the meeting room. In 1857 J. R. D. Tyssen gave about 400 books on London and guides to other towns.

By 1860 the content of the library was causing concern. The President, Earl Stanhope, complained that 'it should contain all standard works of reference on the special subjects of our studies namely, Antiquities, History and Art. . . At present, being the accumulation of accident rather than design, our library has the most glaring deficiences.'[10] The response was to publish a catalogue in 1861 to help Fellows who lived at a distance, but also in the words of the Preface 'to indicate to Fellows the deficiences, and induce them to supply them from their own libraries'.[11] In the long term Council's decision in 1859 to devote an annual sum 'for the purchase of useful works' instead of occasionally as before, was more significant. The library was estimated to contain some 10,000 volumes in 1864. The Secretary, Knight Watson reported then that topography was 'the only portion of our Library of which we may justly be proud . . . in other departments, our Library might easily be surpassed by any average Gentleman's Library in the Kingdom'.[12] Topography included the 30,000 or so topographical prints and drawings which make the Society's collection one of the largest in the country after the British Library and the Bodleian. The Society had acquired most of them by the 1860s.[13]

The issue of the 1861 catalogue was succeeded by some considerable donations. The engraver F. W. Fairholt left his books and prints on pageantry in 1866; Albert Way, the former Director, presented his early dictionaries and collection of seal impressions, 1869-74, and in 1869 came the largest bequest of books the Society has received, about 2400 volumes from the architect, Arthur Ashpitel, including some outstanding works by Piranesi and a fine collection of Greek vases.[14]

The Society's premises in Somerset House were becoming too restricted for the growing library, and the government was anxious to acquire the space for the expanding civil service. In 1875, the Society moved to the new apartments provided in Burlington House for the societies formerly in Somerset House together with the Linnean Society and the Royal Society of Chemistry. Three quarters of a mile of shelving allowed what was considered to be sufficient room for expansion, but was mostly occupied by 1910 when the Resident Secretary's accommodation became available for the library. By then, space had to be found for three large donations totalling over 5000 books. G. E. Cockayne, Clarenceux Herald, gave over 1000 books on heraldry in 1895.

Two years later, Sir Augustus Wollaston Franks, President, left all his books on antiquities, art, history and genealogy that were not already in the library and his heraldic manuscripts; he had earlier given 800 books and a large collection of brass rubbings. New catalogues or supplements were printed in 1868, 1887 and 1899 to incorporate this material. From 1900 to 1902, the library of the Royal Archaeological Institute was dispersed with the Society receiving about 2000 items on archaeology and history not already held. Members of the Institute were granted reading rights in return. The libraries of the Society for the Promotion of Hellenic Studies and the Anthropological Institute, which were offered on the same terms in 1901, were refused because of lack of space.[15]

Growth has been more steady for most of the twentieth century. The one exception was Kelmscott Manor, William Morris's country house in Oxfordshire, which eventually came to the Society with its contents in 1962. Most of Morris's own library had been sold after his death in 1896, but the manor contained the library of his daughters, Jane who died in 1935 and May who died in 1938. Many volumes are inscribed by William Morris and the collection includes his 1475 edition of Alexander of Hales, which he took to his paper manufacturer, J. Batchelor, as a guide for making paper for the Kelmscott Press, the tools he designed for the special Doves binding of the Kelmscott Chaucer, the sixteenth-century Italian writing books which influenced his calligraphy and several of his own calligraphic manuscripts.[16] The most recent bequest of rare books has been that of A. W. G. Lowther in 1972. About 1600 Civil War tracts and some books were retained; the remainder sold as falling outside the Society's fields of interest.

More typical of the way in which collections have been built up has been the occasional gift or purchase of an individual item. It has taken 270 years, for example, to acquire all thirteen editions of Camden's *Britannia* issued in England between 1586 and 1806. Edmund Gibson's 1722 edition was one of the Society's first purchases; later editions were presented when they were published. Apart from the 1590 *Britannia*, given in 1727, these were the only copies in the library until 1868. In the following ten years six of the earliest editions were given by Fellows. The only one missing, that of 1610, was purchased in 1993.[17]

The three miles of shelving in the library today contain about 150,000 books and 500 current periodicals as well as manuscripts, prints and drawings. The Society has an acquisitions policy agreed in 1991 which limits the items purchased to a greater extent than before. Gifts are always welcomed as long as those not required for the library can be disposed of at the Librarian's discretion. They usually number 200 to 300 each year and continue the close association between antiquaries and their library which has been maintained over nearly 300 years.

References

1. The fullest history of the Society is J. Evans, *A History of the Society of Antiquaries of London* (1956). The growth of the library is outlined in R. Bruce-Mitford, *The Society of Antiquaries of London: notes on its history and possessions* (1951), and J. Hopkins, 'The Society of Antiquaries and its library', *Libraries Bulletin* (University of London), no.9, (Jan/Mar 1977), pp.5-8. The most important donations of books are noted in M. Williams (ed.), *A Directory of rare books and special collections in the United Kingdom and the Republic of Ireland* (1985, 2nd ed. by B. Bloomfield forthcoming 1996).
2. Society of Antiquaries of London (SAL), *Minutes*, vol.I, p.17, 24 December 1718; *Minutes*, vol.I, p.28, 16 December 1719.
3. C. Kortholt, *De societe antiquaria Londinensi* (Leipzig, 1735).
4. SAL, *Minutes*, vol.VII, p.135, 20 June 1754.
5. SAL, *Ants. Papers*, 7 Nov 1754, Henry Baker.
6. SAL, *Minutes*, vol.VIII, fol.21, 5 May 1757; R. Lemon, *Catalogue of a collection of printed broadsides in the possession of the Society of Antiquaries of London* (1866); W. A. Jackson, 'Humphrey Dyson's Library', *Papers of the Bibliographical Society of America*, 43 (1949), pp.279-87; K. F. Pantzer, 'Ephemera in the STC revision: a housekeeper's view', *Printing History*, 4 (1982), pp.34-6; J. Evans, *A History* (1956), p.71 for the origins of the broadsides collection in Stukeley's proposal of 1725.
7. SAL, *Minutes*, vol.XI, pp.5-8, 12 Jan 1769.
8. G. R. Tashjian *et al.*, *Richard Rawlinson, a tercentenary memorial* (Western Michigan University, 1990), pp.62-7; J. Evans, *A History* (1956), pp.127-8.
9. N. Carlisle, *A Catalogue of printed books in the library of the Society of Antiquaries* (1816); H. Ellis, *A Catalogue of manuscripts in the library of the Society of Antiquaries* (1816). A new catalogue of manuscripts is in preparation, the only one since 1816.
10. *Proceedings of the Society of Antiquaries of London*, 2nd series, 1, p.140, 23 April 1860.
11. *List of printed books in the library of the Society of Antiquaries* (1861).
12. C. Knight Watson, 'Report on the state of the library', *Proceedings of the Society of Antiquaries of London*, 2nd series, 3 (1864), p.7.
13. M. Barley, *A Guide to British topographical collections* (1974).
14. [C. S. Perceval], *Catalogue of the collection of works on pageantry bequeathed to the Society of Antiquaries by the late Frederick William Fairholt* (1869); *Proceedings of the Society of Antiquaries of London*, 2nd series, 6 (1874), pp.207-12 (list of dictionaries given by Way).
15. J. Evans, *A History* (1956), p.362; Royal Archaeological Institute, *Catalogue of the library* (1890).

16. A. R. Dufty, 'William Morris and the Kelmscott Estate', *Antiquaries Journal*, 43 (1963), pp.97-115; inscription in Alexander de Ales, *Super tertium Sentiarum* (Venice, 1475), SAL Incunabula 2; M. Tidcombe, *The Doves Bindery* (1991), pp.53-7; A. Osley, 'William Morris's Italian writing books', *Antiquaries Journal* 64 (1984), pp.351-60; B. Rosenbaum (ed.), *Index of English literary manuscripts*, IV, part 3 (1993), pp.473-747.
17. E. B. Nurse, 'The 1610 edition of Camden's *Britannia*', *Antiquaries Journal*, 73 (1993), pp.158-60.

Index

Aberdeen, Lord, 74
Abbey, Major J. R., 2, 130
Aelfric
— Homilies, 74
— Society, 74
Aethelwold, St, Benedictional of, 75
Agnese, portolan atlas, 141-2, 145
Akbar Nama, 135, 145
Alexander, Professor J. J. G., 130,
  131
Althorp, Northants, 107
Anglo-Saxon texts, 73
Archaeologia, 46, 73, 75
Arenberg, Dukes of, 141
Arnold, Thomas, 79
Ashpitel, Arthur, 155
Aubrey, John, 61
Auvray, Baron, 136

Backhouse, Janet, vi, 113-28
Bedford Hours and Psalter, 76, 113,
  117, 119, 120, 123, 125, 127
Bell, Harold Idris, 120, 121, 123, 124
Bening, Simon, 144
Bentham, Rev James, 60
Beowulf, 73
Beres, Pierre, 132
Bever, Thomas, 50, 51
'Bibliomania', 83, 85, 97, 98, 108
Bibliophily, 24
Bill, William, 35
Birrell, Professor T. A., vi, 71-82
Binski, Paul, 77
Bisse, Philip, 3, 13, 14, 17, 20
Blackwood, William, 97
Blandford, Marquess of, 97, 98
Blundell, Richard Shireburn Weld,
  122
Blunt, Anthony, 130
Bodley, Thomas, 4

Bollandists, 71, 105 *see also* Book sales
Bookbindings
— armorial, 13, 30, 35, 37
— black-on-white, 22
— blind-stamped, 17, 20, 32
— cheap structures, 32, 35
— collections of, 2
— colours of, 36, 38
— decorated, 9, 12, 13, 14, 17, 20, 22,
  30, 32, 38
— Designer Bookbinders, 7
— endbands, 28
— endleaves, 10, 11, 27, 38
— gilt-tooled, 17, 20, 35, 39
— headbands, 40
— in Bamberg, 28-30
— in Bologna, 35
— in Cambridge, 1, 17, 32
— in London, 1, 4, 17, 20
— in Oxford, 1-26, 32, 33
— in Paris, 9, 35
— instructions for binding, 9
— interim structures, 28
— King Edward and Queen Mary
  binder, 35
— lacing in, 32
— leaf edges, 19, 20, 21, 30, 37, 39, 40
— leatherbound, 12, 28, 38, 39
— lettering, 41
— marbled paper, 39
— materials used for, 32
— Middle Hill, 14
— monastic, 28, 30
— panel stamps, 18
— paper used in, 32, 39
— pasteboard, 32, 39
— pastedowns, 11
— patterns, 5
— publishers', 28
— ready-bound, 20, 27